Moody·Nolan

Aesthetics Function Technology

Preface by
Curtis J. Moody,
FAIA, NCARB, NOMA

Introduction by
Robert Livesey,
FAIA

l'ARCAEDIZIONI

*We would like to thank
Danielle Ford, Judy Kienle
and Molly Grannan Maloof
for their kind collaboration.*

Chief Editor of Collection
Maurizio Vitta

Publishing Coordinator
Franca Rottola

Editorial Staff
Cristina Rota

Graphic Design
Monica Fumagalli - Iliprandi Associati

Editing and Translation
Aaron Maines

Colour-separation
LitofilmsItalia, Bergamo

Printing
Bolis Poligrafiche SpA, Azzano San Paolo (BG)

First published December 2002

Copyright 2002
by l'Arca Edizioni

ISBN 88-7838-144-6

Contents

Aesthetics Function Technology

by Curtis J. Moody, FAIA, NCARB, NOMA

Our designs must be an interpretative expression of our clients' programmatic needs.
Form, function, technology, light, texture and image are all factors in providing exceptional design; however, we must also address context, timelessness, and the cultural expression of art.

Moody and Associates opened in the spring of 1982 at 35 South Champion Avenue, Columbus, Ohio with the help of two investors and previous employers of mine, Lee Brubaker, AIA and Kent Brandt, AIA. Ohio General Corporate Law at that time mandated that only an architect could own interest in an architectural firm. I was very fortunate that those two men saw something in me worthy of their investment.

Moody and Associates began operations with me as jack-of-all-trades and a young female graduate architect serving as secretary and office support. Our first commission was New Life Apostolic Church for a fee of $10,000 and a very tight $150,000 construction budget. Our first business challenge, however, was merely surviving in a highly competitive marketplace that had not been kind to firms of similar ethnic orientation. It was evident during the 1980's that there were societal misconceptions that prevented minority architects from having a major role in large civic projects. At that time, minority architects were employed mostly in supportive roles and rarely in leadership roles. As a result, there were few large minority-owned firms and the minority classification was one given regardless of one's education or abilities.

By the end of our first year of business, we had grown to nine staff members. Howard E. Nolan, P.E. had just left his job as Assistant Director of Transportation for the State of Ohio to establish his own firm of Howard E. Nolan and Associates Civil Engineers. He also employed one support person. After sub-leasing from me at the Champion Avenue site, it became apparent to both of us that a partnership might give both of us the best chance of success.

In 1984, Howard E. Nolan purchased the interest of the original investors, Lee Brubaker and Ken Brandt, and the firm name was changed to Moody/Nolan Ltd., Inc.

After experiencing firsthand that we were perceived as less than equal, it became very apparent to both of us that the evolution of our firm would need to go beyond the traditional path of minority firms. First, we would need to challenge the cultural and societal trends that had stereotyped us and evolve into a firm that represented the best in our field regardless of our ethnicity. We would have to do this by providing exemplary services, designing signature projects and hiring the most capable people regardless of racial background. Our firm would truly have to represent diversity before it was popular.

The modest success that we have been fortunate to receive was not achieved solely by our own efforts. Prayer and faith allowed us to begin the journey, and strong-willed pioneering clients made sometimes unpopular decisions to break from the status quo and hire us. Selecting our firm was not always the most socially acceptable decision; however, we truly outworked our competition, provided exceptional service, and created signature designs that proved our clients correct for choosing Moody • Nolan. We remain committed to achieving the highest levels of success for our clients as a tribute to their confidence in our firm.

Our strategy was to develop lines of business that extended our market opportunities. As we tried to expand our outreach, we had to gauge what other services we might offer that would allow us to be more successful in the market place. Our first strategy was to pull the interiors component out of the architectural department and have it operate as its own independent line of business. As years passed, other lines of business followed the same format. Today we have general architecture, sports/recreation architecture, education architecture, healthcare architecture, interior design, civil engineering, dynamic media, and a host of other support services that are within the general architecture structure. We found it necessary to expand our services into the private sector to compete with main line firms that had been successful for decades, and these lines of business allowed us to adjust to the changing marketplace. With our new strategy in place, we could successfully position ourselves for private and public sector work. In 1992, when I was recognized as the national recipient of the Whitney Young, Jr. Award, it helped begin our move from a regional firm to one of national prominence.

In 2002, with a staff of over 130 and a national presence from coast to coast, we still have to overcome some of the original challenges that burdened the firm in 1982. However, we remain positive about the future, and we will succeed as we find those pioneering clients who will continue to hire us on the merits of our work and on the promise that we will stretch their imaginations.

Our commitment is to serving our clients' needs first, by providing a listening ear and a professional response to their program, budget, schedule, and facility needs. It is through this commitment that our clients see Moody • Nolan's many forms of integrity; and although we have done well in the past and currently hold a strong position, our best is yet to come.

Curtis J. Moody, FAIA, NCARB, NOMA is the founding Principal and President/CEO of Moody • Nolan, Inc.

An Expanded Vision of Practice

by Robert Livesey, FAIA

Founded by Curtis Moody, FAIA, and Howard Nolan, PE, as an architectural/engineering practice, Moody • Nolan has from the start been multidisciplinary and inclusive. From day one, their mission has been to provide a service to their clients and to act as exemplary role models of leadership and integrity in the community.

Curt Moody established his architectural firm in 1982. After a distinguished career with the Ohio Department of Transportation, Howard Nolan established his own firm in 1983. In 1984, the two formed a partnership with Moody • Nolan, uniting a depth of experience that enabled the firm to move into areas of opportunities neither could accomplish alone. Howard characterizes the nature of their relationship by quoting a friend's favorite saying, "A partnership is even closer than a marriage. If the compatibility isn't there, it fails." As testimony to their success, the firm is approaching the celebration of its twentieth anniversary.

Howard Nolan was raised in Dayton, Ohio and earned a Bachelor of Science degree in architectural engineering from Ohio University. Prior to establishing Moody • Nolan, Howard and Curt worked as a team of independent contractors to design the MRI Laboratory at The Ohio State University. Working within a defined budget and with a requirement to use nonferrous materials in the project, the team faced enormous challenges. They surpassed the client's expectations by developing a new material for the MRI Laboratory. Their innovation for using a nonferrous type of shielding not only won the client's favor; it has become the standard shielding used in these facilities today.

The client's positive feedback about the synergy between the two principals in this project, combined with the suggestion that obtaining future projects would be easier if the two had a "closer relationship," led to the formalization of Moody • Nolan. With Curt and Howard sharing the same vision and values, it was a natural union. They also shared other commonalities: neither was afraid of the responsibility of leading a company and both wanted to be entrepreneurs who owned their own building. At the time there existed a general perception that minority firms were not capable of handling larger projects. Moody • Nolan dispelled that notion so often that it ceased to be an issue. In addition, as part of Curt's and Howard's dream, they purchased and renovated a 10,000 sq. ft. building for their offices. Although Howard Nolan retired in 1999; these commitments remain firm today under Curt Moody's leadership.

Moody • Nolan is at once the vision of an individual and the work of a team. It might be too simple to say that to understand Curt Moody is to understand the firm. However, it can be no accident that the firm expresses much of his personality and experience. Curt Moody grew up in Columbus, Ohio, test market capital of the country and a place where manners and respect for others are deemed important. Curt's childhood aspirations were to play basketball and go to college. As he developed an interest in architecture, he was discouraged from aspiring to be an architect. However, Curt was determined. He persevered and applied to the School of Architecture at The Ohio State University. He could have picked no better place to encounter the challenges of a rigorous architecture curriculum and a demanding basketball program.

At Ohio State one could see the nucleus of what would later develop as one of the most successful firms in Central Ohio. From architecture, Curt gained the knowledge he needed to be an architect, and from basketball he learned the importance of drills, the ability to direct a team, and the necessity of listening to the coach. These are not small skills, and they have contributed significantly to the firm's meteoric rise in the profession.

Architects are sometimes thought to be arrogant and aloof. Not Moody • Nolan. One presumes that the firm's dedication to the client comes from Curt's Midwest background and his early days as a player/student. There are at least two qualities of the firm's work that seem directly related. First, no normal human being could possibly juggle the demands of architecture and basketball at OSU. Curt had to learn early to listen carefully and focus on the essentials. As a result, one of the qualities of Moody • Nolan's work is its attention to programmatic needs. Second, as a point guard on the basketball team, Curt learned to be the leader in the middle. He directed the players on the floor, but he was implementing the coach's call from the side. Up to the most recent work, little has changed except that the client has replaced the coach.

At the risk of overplaying the basketball analogy, it is interesting to note how Curt advanced the firm in its early years. In order to undertake substantial projects on its own, Moody • Nolan associated with other well established firms. Those firms both provided coaching and allowed Moody • Nolan to focus on developing specific skills. Most notable among these projects was the design of the exterior skins for the Riffe Tower and the Columbus Convention Center.

It was a brilliant strategy that could be easily associated with doing basketball drills. The all-around player/firm is a product of developing and then combining individual skills. In the work, it is easy to see these skills improve over time.

For all the talk about coaching, there is no getting around the necessity of talent and the self-confidence to apply it. From the beginning Moody • Nolan has been a talented firm. The improved quality of the work has come with increased self-confidence. Nowhere is this more evident than Port Columbus International Airport. As the architects for the airport, they have undertaken three projects: the South Terminal in 1990, the North Terminal in 1995, and the North Terminal extension in 2002. While the first expansion is accommodating, it is not memorable. On the other hand, the latest addition is filled with light and carefully articulated; the seating areas are intimate; the retail spaces are made as objects to enliven the concourse, and the circulation space is grand.

Moody • Nolan's self-confidence has also come from doing "building drills": designing the same or similar building types over and over again. However, they have not merely improved their skills; they have changed their relationship with the client. The client now comes to them as the authority. The firm has graduated from being a player to being the coach.

The final component of the basketball analogy is the fans. In architectural terms, the fans are the community. The mission of the firm has always been:"to serve the client and the community." Therefore, it is not surprising to see recurring community themes as driving forces in the work. For instance, the use of a public space as an organizing device and a respect for the context are consistent qualities of all the work. One of the firm's earliest projects in which community issues were made explicit was the renovation of an old warehouse building for the Martin Luther King Center for the Performing Arts in Columbus. Since the building itself was a community facility, the firm's penchant for including public space was transferred to the outside by adding a plaza and park to the neighborhood. In addition, a street was added to fix the access disrupted by the insertion of an interstate highway.

In 1989 the firm was commissioned to design a series of neighborhood libraries. Basically, the buildings were infill projects ranging from urban to suburban. Although the firm was doing larger-scale projects at the time; this was a scale that they had clearly mastered. Each library is different,

but all have the same elements: an identifiable entry piece, a community room, a double height organizing spine, and a garden room. As if to highlight Moody • Nolan's skill at performing drills, each of the buildings, in a different way, is at once the focus and a microcosm of its neighborhood.

The concurrent timing of the Dresse Laboratory at Ohio State, the Recreation Sports Facility at Miami University and the UAW/Ford Motor Company Training Center at Lima Technical College with the library projects proved a stretch for the firm. The shear volume of programs dwarfs any attempts to articulate the building elements. The buildings' masses lose the distinctions that were so clear in the libraries. However, the jump in scale of these projects is critical for the firm's advancement. Having shot from 30 feet, the next drill from 20 feet must seem relatively easy.

Indeed, in the next series of medium-scaled projects, the firm does resolve the building elements in Davidson Hall at Columbus State Community College, the Conroe (Texas) Regional Medical Center, the Olympic Preliminary Basketball Venue at Morehouse College, the Library and Classroom building at Ohio State, Marion. The lesson is clear. The material palette at Morehouse and Ohio State, Marion are much more refined than earlier projects. The layering of the façade and the public amenity space in Davidson Hall are both pronounced and emblematic of the building. However, these buildings do not represent the end of investigations. For instance, the volumetric cylinder tower introduced at Ohio State, Marion is later seen at the Schottenstein Center.

There can be little question that the Jerome Schottenstein Center at The Ohio State University was the "big game" for Moody • Nolan. It has everything. All that practice with masonry buildings is now combined with metal; all that practice with public spaces is now absolutely necessary to move the crowds; all that practice with intimately scaled spaces is used in the viewing suites and Huntington Club; and, of course, all that practice on entrance towers is now done in a monumental scale. The building is more than a display of learned skills. It shows that Moody • Nolan can put those lessons to work in a coherent whole. Most importantly, the success here builds the firm's self-confidence.

The firm's new abilities are best illustrated in the next series of projects. First is the UAW/Ford Motor Training Center. Located at a manufacturing facility, this building is all business. Tightly planed and tautly skinned, it is clearly drawing on the lessons learned at the "Schott." Although the Nationwide Parking Garage is primarily a façade project; it is much more assertive than might have been expected earlier. The public amenity "space" is compressed onto a public outdoor projection screen. The Jesse Owens Memorial Stadium at Ohio State is a façade given a third dimension. The corner entrance pavilions are separated as trophies for the victors, and there is a definite confidence about the mix of materials.

If there is any question about the firm's increasing sophistication, one need only note the difference between the layering of the façades at the Hampton University Student Center and Columbus State. The latter is much more controlled. Both the mix of materials and the form of the building at Cincinnati State Technical College seem much more directed and intentional. However, the Student Recreational Center at West Virginia University is the real leap forward. Here what was once surface has become volumetric, what was once adjacency has become a tightly organized plan, and what were once applied materials have been used to reduce the building's scale.

There are other projects now on the boards where these skills and themes are carried forward. However, there can be no question that we are seeing the firm midstride and that no matter how good or competent the current work may be, this is a firm that is always listening and learning. It is now in a position to push a unique and developed notion of practice to a new level. One is also confident that Moody • Nolan will not forget its roots, but include these new principles in an expanded vision of practice.

Robert Livesey, FAIA
Director of Knowlton School of Architecture
The Ohio State University

Works

Port Columbus International Airport

**Columbus, Ohio,
1990-2002**

Client
Port Columbus
International Airport

Principal in Charge
Curtis J. Moody, FAIA

Project Manager
Steven C. Glass, AIA

Interior Designer
David C. Miller

*Construction
Administrator*
Arthur N. Cox

Photographer
Brad Feinknopf, Owen
Smithers

In 2001, approximately 3.4 million passengers used Port Columbus International Airport in Columbus, Ohio, many of them passing through numerous additions designed by Moody • Nolan. Since 1990, this firm provided two terminal expansions, an escalator addition, retail space additions, and interior design services as part of a design-build team with Turner Construction and Gresham Smith Engineers.

The South Terminal Expansion, a 106,000 sq. ft. airport addition, included six gates for full-size aircraft, a new baggage handling system, offices, shops, and storage areas for the principal tenant, USAir. During this expansion, the designer developed a new escalator addition creating a focal point for the main terminal. The goals of this project were to design two escalator additions connecting three floors and create entry design features and respect for the Veterans Memorial Courtyard. The design provided two glass drum enclosures that overlook the plaza and serve as landings for the escalators. With these new features, the escalator maintains the existing entry traffic pattern, while upgrading its image and function.

In addition, the firm also provided complete design services for a new 1,600 sq. ft. retail space devoted to sports apparel and accessories for the "Big 10" schools. Eleven wall fixture units frame two sides of the space, providing identical displays for each of the school's signature items. The third side and the curved cash-wrap area feature displays devoted to local teams, in this case, The Ohio State Buckeyes. This test store design gained overwhelming approval and was slated to be the model for rollouts in all of the "Big 10" cities.

A new 4,000 sq. ft. store comprised of three separate and distinct, high-end retail spaces for the retailer, Paradies, was another of the firm's designs at Port Columbus International Airport. The retail spaces include The PGA Tour Shop, Heritage Book Sellers, and the Broad & High Emporium, a prototype for a gift, clothing, and sundries retailer. The Emporium recreates a mid-western street scene using actual brick building façades, and features a "Theater" and a "Diner" as backdrops for Columbus, Ohio merchandise and apparel.

The North Terminal project, the last of the expansions, was built in two phases and added nine gates, as outlined in the airport master plan created by the firm. Phase I of the expansion included a four-gate, three-story, 130,000 sq. ft. addition, the first high ceiling space in this airport. The building is a distinctive destination in the airport featuring a third floor, large clerestory window, curved roof, and an atrium designed to bring light into the terminal. Food service, concessions, and retail space were also components of this project.

Phase II of the North Terminal project brought the airport up to new standards with five additional gates, new hold rooms, airline operations, and new baggage handling systems.

Moody • Nolan earned a 1992 National Association of Minority Architects (NOMA) Honor Award for the airport terminal expansions.

Above, night view of
North Terminal.
Right, computer
rendering of final phase
development of North
Terminal.
Opposite page,
Expansion of North
Terminal Concourse
"C".

Right from top, South Terminal expansion's baggage claim area; South Terminal expanded ticket counter and concourse area. Opposite page, South Terminal night view.

Livingston Avenue Branch Library

Columbus, Ohio, 1992

Client
Columbus Metropolitan Library

Principal in Charge
Curtis J. Moody, FAIA

Project Manager
Amalia Iglesias

Interior Designer
Eileen M. Goodman, NCIDQ

Construction Administrator
William C. Reinehr, EIT

Photographers
Todd B. Dove, Leslee Kass, Owen Smithers

Voters passed a levy to support building this new 12,000 sq. ft, suburban branch of the Columbus Metropolitan Library. The levy also calls for building other new branches, each distinctive in design, and built according to the Columbus Metropolitan Library system's program for all regional branches. This suburban branch is located on Livingston Avenue, a major commercial thoroughfare adjacent to a residential area in Columbus, Ohio. The design challenge included developing street presence in the face of major parking challenges. New parking is located on the west side of the building due to site restrictions, and adjacent to this new parking area is one of the public bus transportation system's park-and-ride lots.

To address the issue of developing an attractive street presence, the designer created a new entry rotunda that is visible from both the parking area and the main street and orients patrons to library services, meeting spaces, and rest rooms. The library is organized along a central spine linking the front entrance to a lounge located in the rear of the building. Along this path, various library functions are located in "chapels" of space. A tall clerestory gallery defined by a parallel row of columns highlights the spine. Lighting is also an integral design element in the library, with skylights at the center of each bay, wall sconces, and cove lighting, creating a great area to enjoy the library's many services.

Exterior design elements that make this structure distinctive include brick in two colors, windows in various sizes, clerestory windows, and color on the window frames. The rooflines also complement the design and mimic the residential structures of the adjacent neighborhood.

Moody • Nolan met with community members multiple times to assure them of having a "one-of-a-kind" facility.

This project earned a 1992 Ohio Association of Minority Architects and Engineers (OAMAE) Honor Award.

Right from top, west elevation facing parking area; south elevation main entry rotunda. Opposite page from left, main circulation spine and children's area.

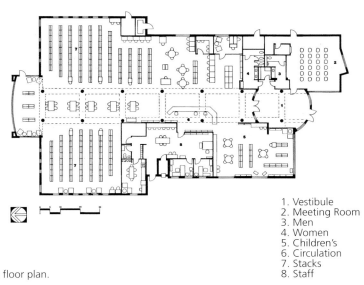

Main floor plan.

1. Vestibule
2. Meeting Room
3. Men
4. Women
5. Children's
6. Circulation
7. Stacks
8. Staff

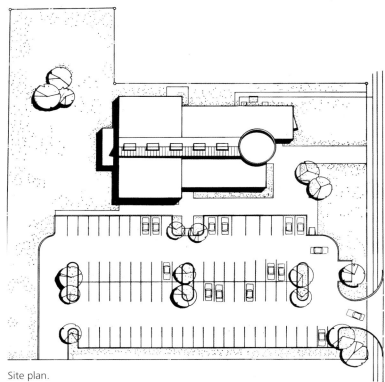

Site plan.

West elevation.

South elevation.

North elevation.

Dreese Laboratory at The Ohio State University

Columbus, Ohio, 1994

Client
The Ohio State University

Principal in Charge
Curtis J. Moody, FAIA

Project Manager
Robert K. Larrimer, AIA

Interior Designer
Eileen M. Goodman, NCIDQ

Construction Administrator
Dennis Keller

Photographers
Owen Smithers, Leslee Kass

The Ohio State University College of Engineering and the Department of Computer Science, having outgrown their spaces, combined resources to create a 105,000 sq. ft., nine-story addition that supports two of the most technically advanced research laboratories in collegiate ranks.

These special purpose laboratories include a clean room for the development of one-of-a-kind computer chips and a high voltage laboratory. The advanced capabilities of the high voltage laboratory provide opportunities for research and development but can interfere with computer systems. Since both the laboratories and computer science rooms share the facility, the designer lined the walls with copper to protect the computer systems from radioactive wave interference. In addition to the laboratories, the facility houses administrative offices, conference rooms, a data processing center, classrooms, and a faculty lounge.

The challenges in this project were in the architectural details of the exterior. Matching the new vertical precast and glass curtain wall system with the brick of the existing building was a noteworthy design challenge due to the age of the brick on the existing facility. New windows in the addition did not match the windows of the existing building; therefore, all old windows were replaced and updated to match. The designer housed the chillers on the roof in innovative, lighted enclosures that provide ventilation and visual interest. This design complements the University skyline and creates an attractive view from the faculty lounge that overlooks this building.

While many projects are closely supervised, this project was subject to a different kind of scrutiny— that of the University's architect whose office overlooked the construction site. As expected, the project was completed on time and under budget.

Right, northeast tower
entry.
Opposite page, view
looking northwest.

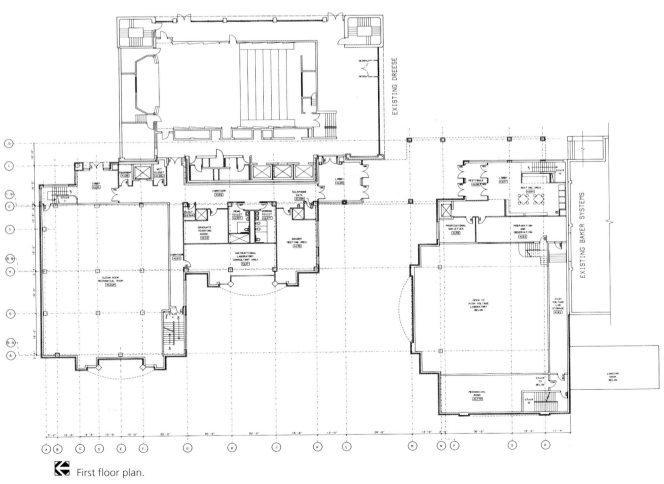

First floor plan.

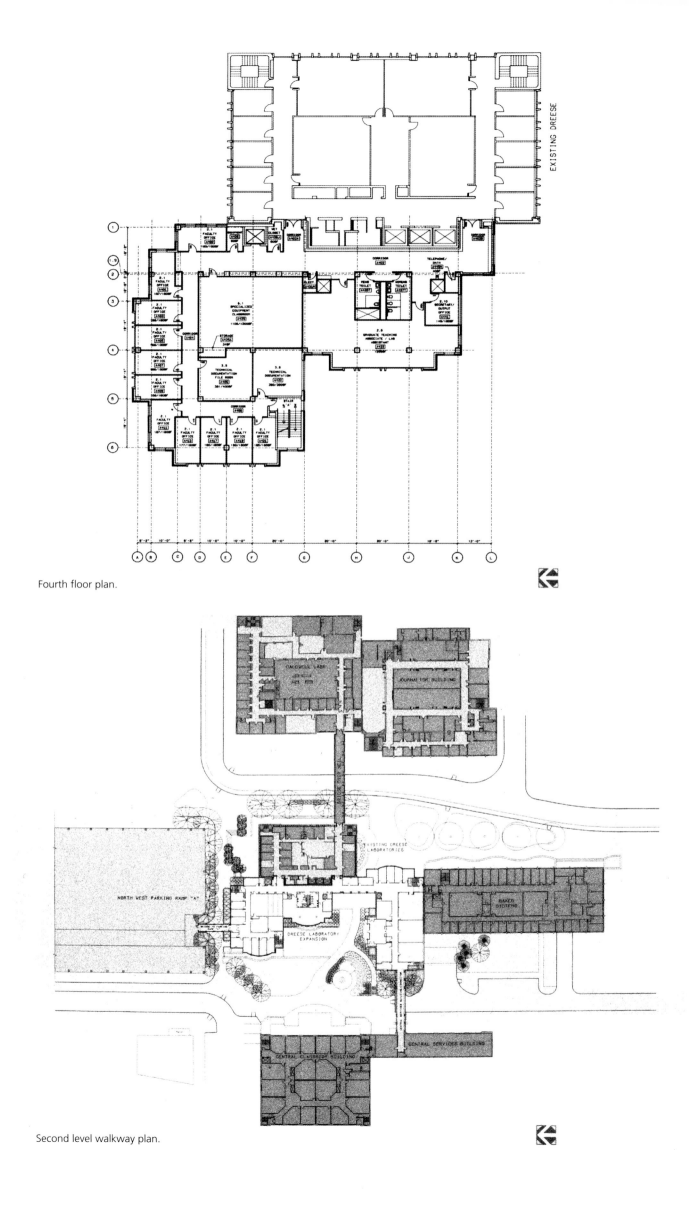

Fourth floor plan.

Second level walkway plan.

Faculty lounge and tower observation deck.

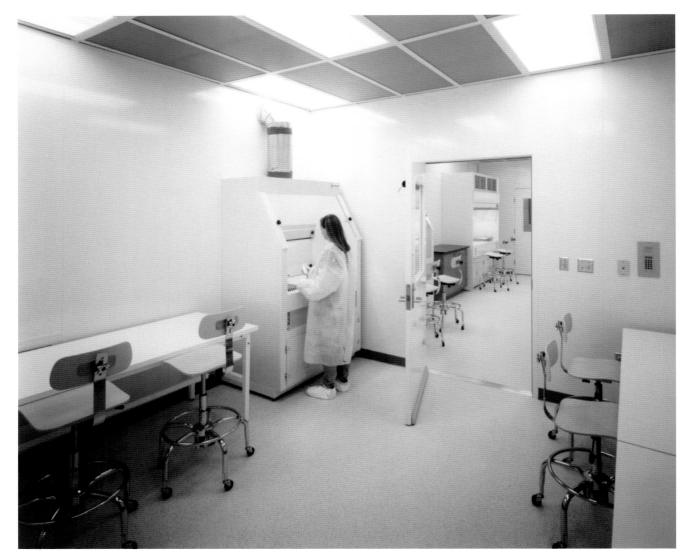

Right, views of two of the five clean rooms housed in Dreese Laboratory.
Opposite page, typical classroom.

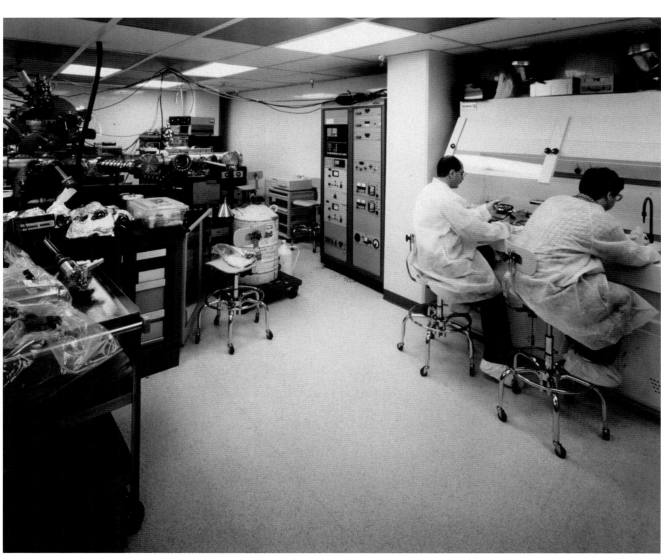

UAW/Ford Motor Company Training Center at Lima Technical College

Lima, Ohio, 1995

Client
Lima Ford Engine Plant

Principal in Charge
Curtis J. Moody, FAIA

Project Manager
Ronald C. Minekime, AIA

Interior Designer
Eileen M. Goodman, NCIDQ

Construction Administrator
William L. Kemper

Photographers
Owen Smithers, Leslee Kass

Economic changes and the increasing use of robotics and computerized equipment to build engines forced The United Auto Workers (UAW) and Ford Plant in Lima, Ohio to begin retraining autoworkers to use new technology. With the assistance of Lima Technical College, UAW and Ford developed a program to address these changes and the evolving needs of their workforce.

Ford Engine Plant, assisted by state funding, now features an expanded plant that includes a new training facility. The objective of the expansion was to create a facility on the inside that would address the 21st century training needs of autoworkers and still tie into the industrial look of the existing plant's exterior. Owners also wanted to encourage the community to use the new auditorium when it was not needed for work force retraining.

With the expansion in place, the Ford Plant, a natural choice for a training facility, now includes an auditorium, classrooms, breakout rooms, a library, and a computer laboratory. Distance learning, using technology to connect to other plant locations for training purposes, completes the requirements for the use of this space.

Instead of installing traditional carpeting, this facility is finished with resilient flooring that provides comfort and withstands high volumes of traffic. The finish is also easier to clean in this industrial plant environment.

The silver metal aluminum insulated exterior panels meet the goal of providing a high-tech industrial look to the facility. Using these materials was so successful, the owners reclad the old building to conform to the exterior architecture of the expansion. Glass and precast concrete materials complete the updated industrial design, giving new life to the plant and 21st century training center.

Moody • Nolan won a 1995 National Organization of Minority Architects (NOMA) Design Excellence Award for this project.

Night and daylight views
of main entry atrium
and auditorium exit.
Opposite page, view of
south elevation.

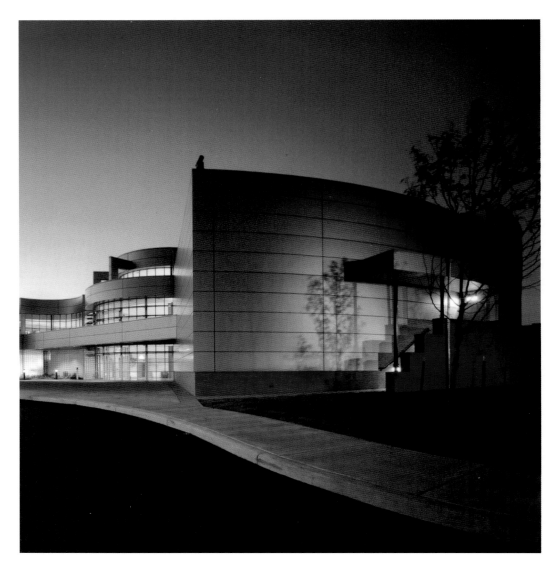

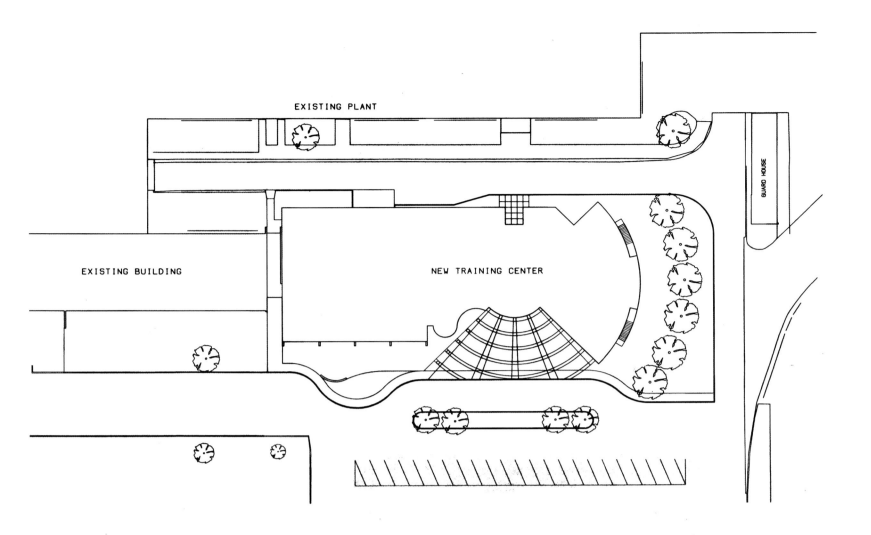

Site plan.

Opposite page from top,
views of the atrium and
of the auditorium.

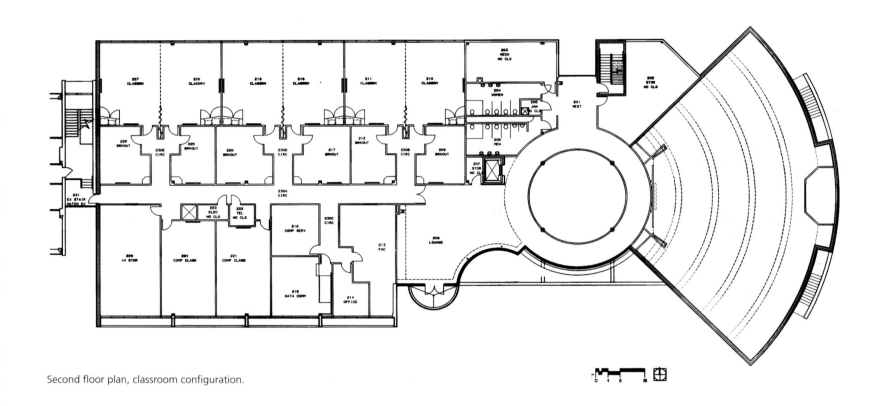

Second floor plan, classroom configuration.

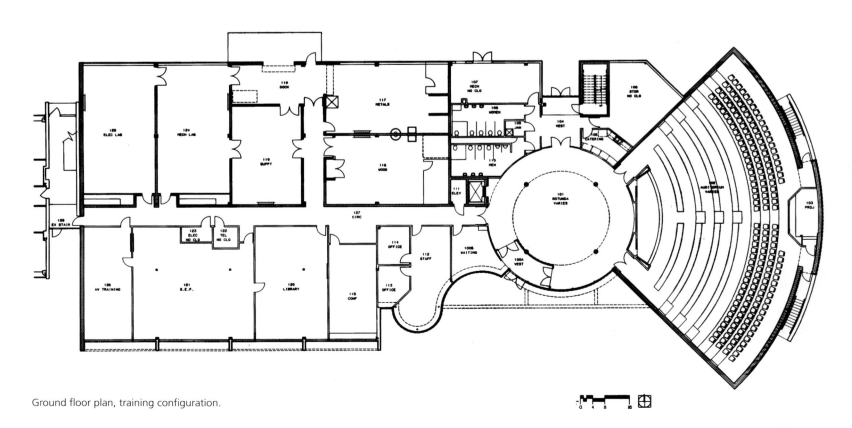

Ground floor plan, training configuration.

Davidson Hall at Columbus State Community College

Columbus, Ohio, 1996

Client
Columbus State
Community College

Principal in Charge
Curtis J. Moody, FAIA

Project Manager
Jack Duran, AIA

Interior Designer
Jill Seitz

Construction Administrator
Paul F. Pryor, AIA

Photographer
Brad Feinknopf

Columbus State Community College is a well-respected and prominent educational institution in Columbus, Ohio with a growing population of nontraditional students seeking a four-year degree program. Moody • Nolan was invited to design Davidson Hall for Columbus State College after previously designing an award-winning building on campus. Working with McDonald, Cassell & Bassett, Moody • Nolan designed a new 75,000 sq. ft. gateway facility that complements the architecture of the first building.

The building includes general-purpose classrooms, computer labs, engineering labs, a greenhouse, math and engineering department offices and a two-level student activity/study lobby. A pedestrian bridge links this new classroom building with a parking garage. The building's design focuses on two highly visible pedestrian areas, the southern and western exposures. The curvilinear design allows the two exposures to be seen as one and provides a strong street presence.

The materials used in the façade are similar to those of other campus buildings, and the volume of glass used in the design corresponds to the scale of the adjacent buildings, creating a harmonious architectural style.

Davidson Hall, with a modest budget and a rigorous completion schedule, is an example of the firm's focus on creating site-specific solutions that reflect the owner's program and budget, while providing design that fits within the context of adjacent space.

This facility is the winner of a 1997 National Organization of Minority Architects (NOMA) Design Excellence Award and a 1997 Builders Exchange Craftsmanship Award.

Opposite page, night view of campus entrance. Left, night view looking east.

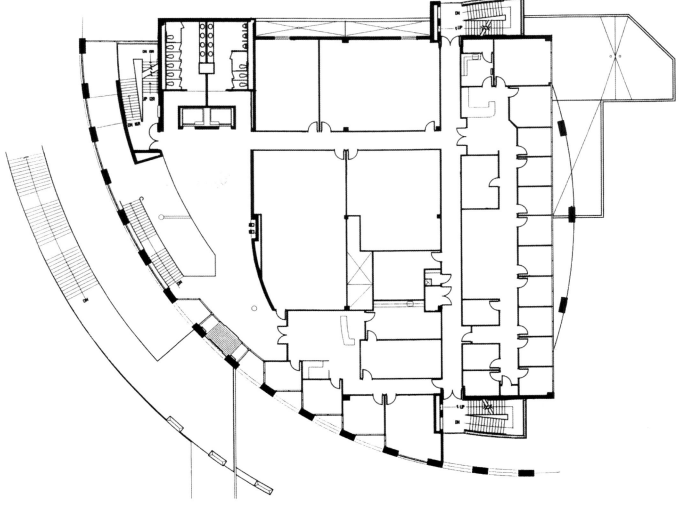

Typical upper floor plan.

Lobby and monumental stair to second floor. Opposite page, view looking west.

Conroe Regional Medical Center

Conroe, Texas, 1996

Client
Health Trust, Inc.

Principal in Charge
Bill Miller, AIA

Project Manager
Aaron Askew

Interior Designer
Michelle Skeie

Construction Administrator
James T. Eckstein, AIA

Photographer
Owen Smithers

Conroe Regional Medical Center is a comprehensive inpatient and outpatient medical surgical care center located in Conroe, Texas. It offers a wide variety of specialty services including a HeartCare Center, a level 3 neonatal intensive care unit, a cancer center, and a nationally recognized center for wound care and hyperbaric medicine. After acquiring new property, Conroe Regional Medical Center decided to reorient the hospital site and build a new entrance.

The new entrance for Conroe Regional Medical Center consists of two three-story medical office buildings with a three-story entrance atriums and a two-story connector to the existing hospital. In addition to the entrance, the cancer center, and the labor, delivery, and recovery areas of the Maternity Department were renovated.

The cancer center, providing chemotherapy and radiation therapy, is located within the 190,000 sq. ft. medical office complex. The gracious and inviting approach, along with the natural beauty of the heavily wooded site, relieves anxiety associated with the typical hospital visit. A water fountain, lanterns and two colors of brick are additional features that aid in softening the monumental scale of the facility and promote a more humane environment.

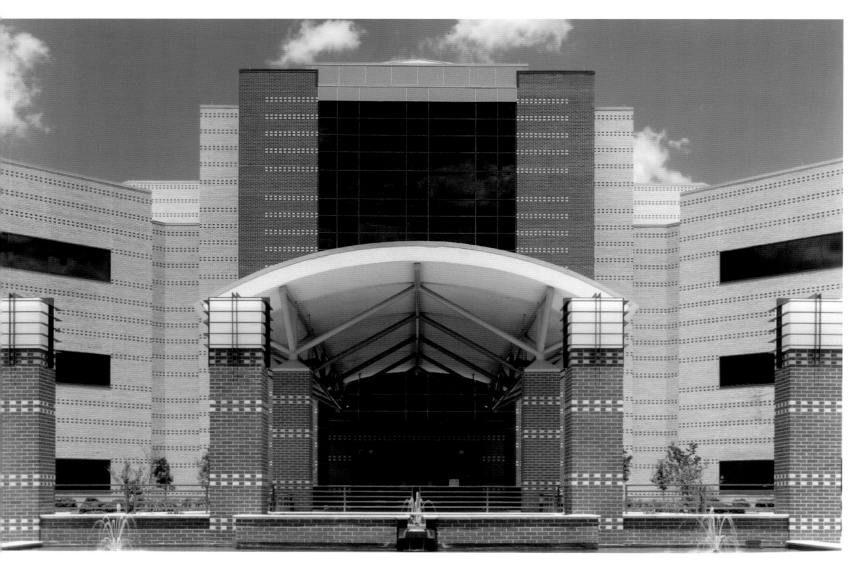

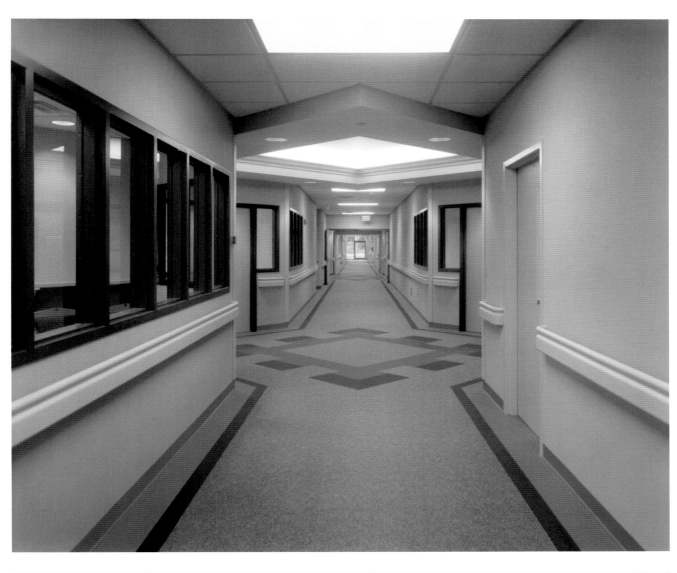

Opposite page from top, grand entrance canopy; view of the lobby/atrium.
Left from top, maternity unit corridor; cancer center radiation room.

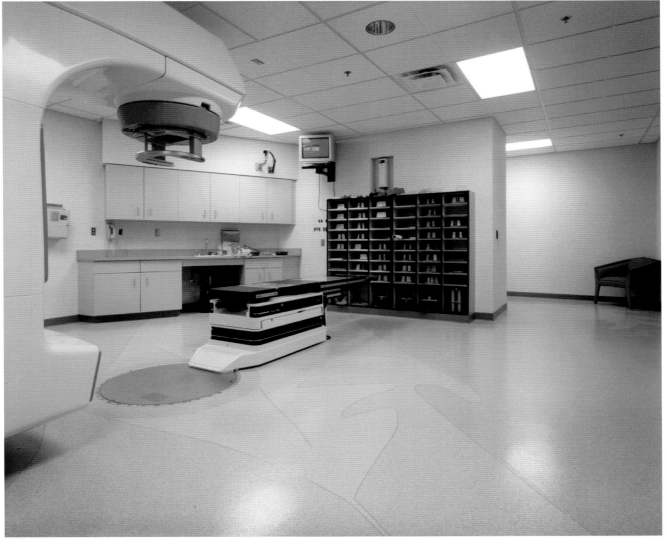

Library and Classroom Building at The Ohio State University

Marion, Ohio, 1996

Client
The Ohio State University

Principal in Charge
Curtis J. Moody, FAIA

Project Manager
Robert K. Larrimer, AIA

Interior Designer
Eileen M. Goodman, NCIDQ

Construction Administrator
William L. Kemper

Photographers
Owen Smithers, Leslee Kass

Marion Technical Institute shares a campus with a branch of The Ohio State University in Marion, Ohio. After conducting a needs assessment planning meeting, the designer recommended the construction of a shared library and classroom facility that would be flexible enough for a variety of uses until future classrooms would be built.

The building, located at the south end of a retention pond, offers a beautiful landscape with a soothing view of the water. The primary design challenge was to create a style that would be compatible with the architecture of future buildings on campus. Adding to this challenge, the design had to meet the expectations of two separate design committees, one from The Ohio State University and the second from Marion Technical Institute, institutions with different needs. Before the final selection of the design, three design directions were submitted and approved by both committees.

The main feature of this library and classroom space is an entry rotunda featuring art that was provided by state-funded art programs. The contemporary design blends with existing campus structures and sets a new standard for the design of future buildings.

In addition to serving the educational institution, the community wholeheartedly endorses the design and uses the facility for a variety of community events and concerts.

This project earned a 1996 National Organization of Minority Architects (NOMA) Design Excellence Award.

Opposite page from top, view of second floor meeting room and night view of main entry. Left from top, public art hung from ceiling in entry rotunda; entry rotunda featuring monumental staircase.

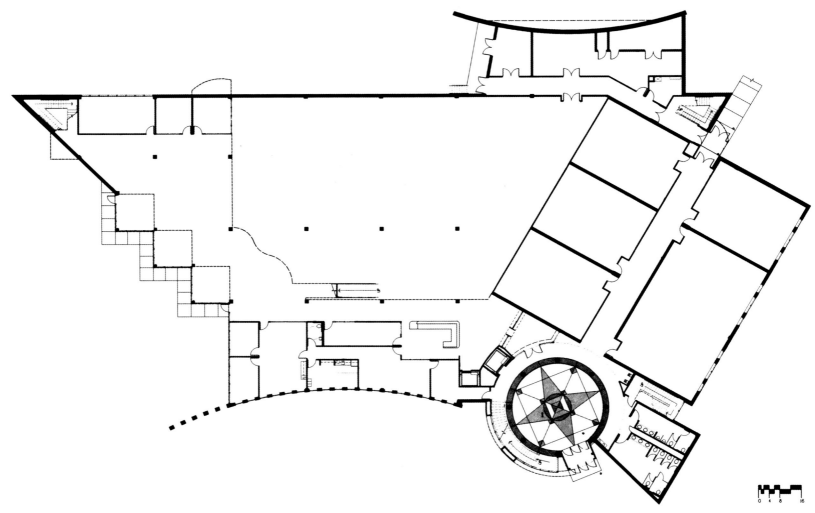

First floor plan.

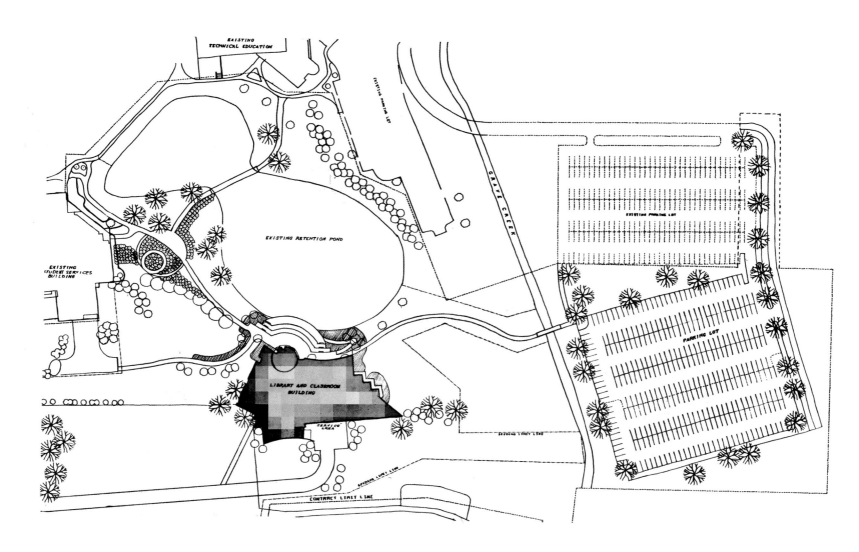

Site plan.

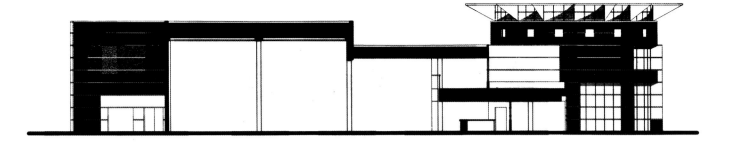

Longitudinal section.

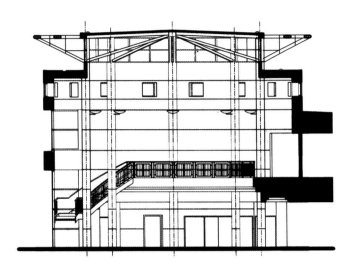

Cross section.

Reading room and stacks area.

Value City Arena at the Jerome Schottenstein Center at The Ohio State University

Columbus, Ohio, 1998

Client
The Ohio State University

Principal in Charge
Curtis J. Moody, FAIA

Project Manager
Robert K. Larrimer, AIA

Project Architect
Ronald C. Minekime, AIA

Interior Designer
Eileen M. Goodman, NCIDQ and William Markland

Construction Administrator
Dennis Keller

Photographers
Brad Feinknopf, Leslee Kass

Moody • Nolan, Lead Designer and Architect of Record, worked with arena design consultant, Sink Combs Dethlefs of Denver, Colorado to design the 700,000 sq. ft. facility. Sasaki Associates Inc. of San Francisco, California assisted the firm with the master plan for this site and those of adjacent facilities. In addition to design services, Moody • Nolan also provided civil engineering services, including the design of over 2,100 parking sites, storm water drainage and detention for a 51-acre site, and roadway improvements. Although the budget for this project was committed years in advance of construction; the firm completed the project on time and within the original budget allocated.

The Value City Arena at The Jerome Schottenstein Center, known locally as the "Schott," is a multipurpose venue for sports, student use, and other events. As host to the men's and women's basketball teams, and the ice hockey team, the facility is one of the few arenas in the country equipped to make either 85 foot or 100 foot Olympic sized ice sheets and converts from a basketball floor to an ice rink in less than four hours.

The arena seats 19,500 for the men's and women's varsity basketball program, 17,000 for ice hockey and up to 21,000 for other special events. Amenities in the building include practice facilities, locker rooms, weight rooms, storage facilities, retail space, private suites with wood paneled doors, sliding glass doors, granite counter tops and a commissary. The designer worked with the Marriott Corporation to provide food service for sports and other events at the arena. The private food service vendor offers a menu different from most sports facilities, featuring special salads, baked Italian calzones, and a more comprehensive menu for patrons using the private suites. A centralized beverage system houses large vats of refreshments in a central location and dispenses them to satellite locations throughout the building, saving valuable space at each dispensing location.

In addiion to receiving accolades for its sports facility capabilities, the arena has also earned national acclaim from notable artists who have performed there. Neil Diamond, after his performance in the "Schott," commented that it was among the best buildings in the country for acoustics. Other testimonials substantiate his claim, and as a result, concerts, shows and other events fill 60% of the scheduled time at the arena.

The arena's open floor plan presented the designer with opportunities to showcase the history of athletics at OSU. The terrazzo floorscape in the lobby, designed by artist Alexis Smith, a focal point of the arena, depicts the schools' great athletes in school colors of scarlet and two shades of gray. Because of the popularity of this design feature, additional money was raised to feature other terrazzo art applications throughout the facility. In addition to terrazzo art, the upper level concourse features a four-foot wide graphic timeline of OSU athletics, from 1880 to the present.

The building, although enormous, has an exterior made of oversized brick to help scale the building and make it compatible with the architecture of adjacent campus buildings. Oversized brick, a rusticated stone base, blue-green glass, and aluminum curtain wall frames are the primary building materials.

Moody • Nolan received five design awards for this project, including a 2000 American Institute of Architects (AIA), Ohio Chapter, Merit Award, a 1999 Builders Exchange Craftsmanship Award, a 1999 Athletic Business Magazine Facility of Merit award, a 1999 Metal Architecture Design Award Honorable Mention, and the 1999 Ohio Golden Trowel Award, Grand Award Winner

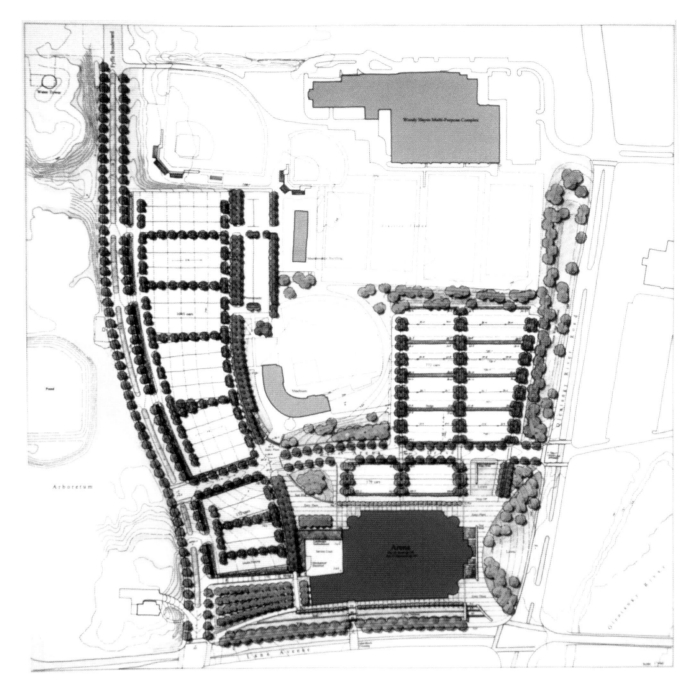

Northwest athletic campus master plan.
Below, view looking northeast.
Opposite page, night view from across Olentangy River.

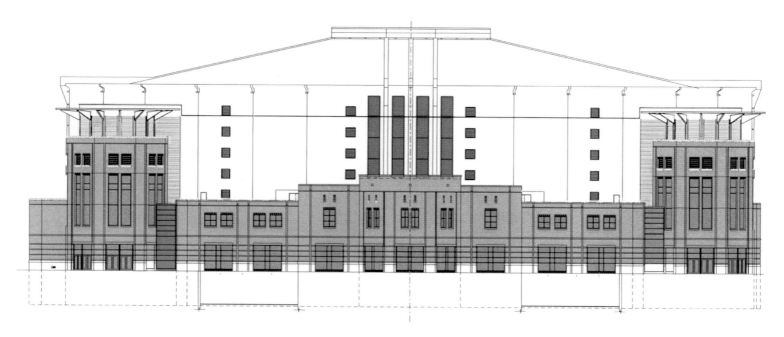

Rear elevation of the building.

Opposite page from top, main pedestrian entrance from campus and detail of rotunda.
Left, Huntington Club lounge.
Below left, Hall of Fame.
Below right, ice hockey floor.

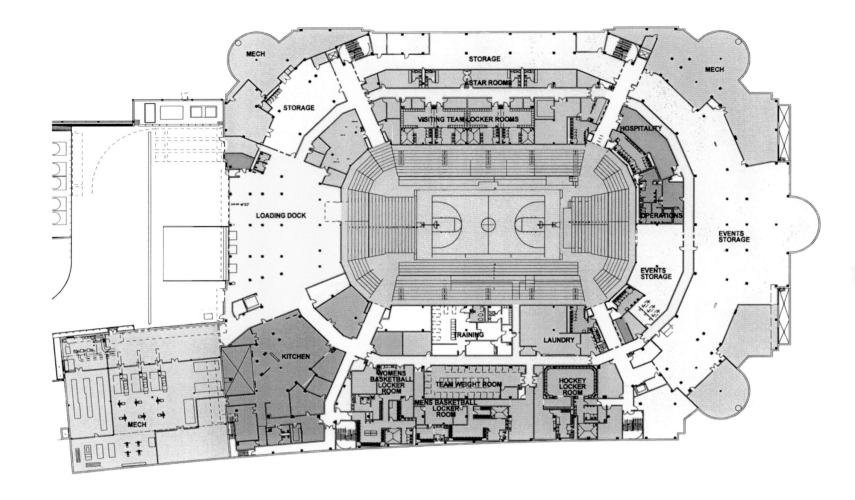

Arena level floor plan.

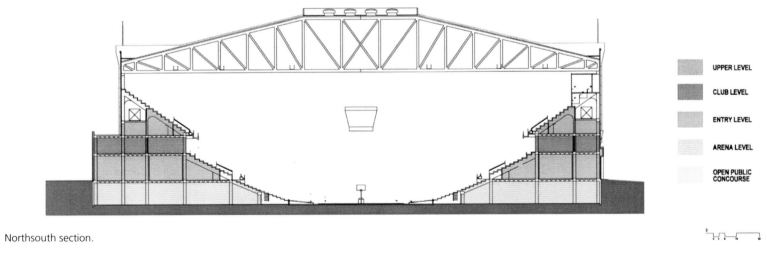

UPPER LEVEL

CLUB LEVEL

ENTRY LEVEL

ARENA LEVEL

OPEN PUBLIC
CONCOURSE

Northsouth section.

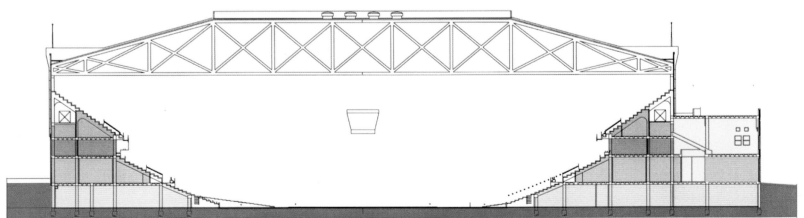

Eastwest section.

Left, men and women varsity athletes' weight training area.
Below left, hockey locker room.
Below right, looking down on bowl area of basketball court.

Office Centers
Gahanna and Polaris

**Gahanna, Ohio,
1998 and
Columbus, Ohio,
1996**

Client
The Daimler Group

Principal in Charge
Curtis J. Moody, FAIA

Project Manager
Steven C. Glass, AIA

Interior Designer
Caren C. Foster

Photographer
D. R. Goff

Moody • Nolan provided architectural design services for two speculative office buildings in Columbus, Ohio for one of the largest developers of office buildings in central Ohio.

The requirements of each office project were to deliver high quality office space within a modest budget. The buildings are predominantly masonry structures with glass covering approximately forty percent of the façade. The remainder of the building exterior is comprised of limestone and precast materials. Both buildings achieved the goals of being attractive, high quality, low maintenance office space.

The Gahanna Office Center includes a matching pair of three-story, 65,000 sq. ft. office buildings. The firm provided site planning, building shell design, design of public spaces, and tenant build-out and construction services for this project.

For the Polaris Office Center, Moody • Nolan provided architectural design services for two speculative office buildings, approximately 100,000 sq. ft. each, that are part of a larger development called the Offices at Polaris.

View of two economical
developer office
buildings.

UAW/Ford MnSCU Training Center

St. Paul, Minnesota, 1999

Client
Ford Motor Company

Principal in Charge
Curtis J. Moody, FAIA

Project Manager
Ronald C. Minekime, AIA

Interior Designer
Caren C. Foster

Photographer
Steven Bergerson Photography

The planning for this 40,000 sq. ft. training center was a joint effort with United Auto Workers Local 879 Ford Motor Company and the State of Minnesota. During an on-site charrette, the architect and engineering team of Toltz, King, Duval, Anderson & Associates and Moody • Nolan developed a building plan that became the basis of this schematic design.

The building is organized into two sections. The public lobby allows general circulation through the building and into the assembly plant. Adjacent to the lobby is an auditorium lecture hall. Classrooms, labs and shop areas are adjacent to the lobby for easy access, but designed to allow separation if needed for safety or lockout during a public event in the lecture hall. The lobby is a two-story space offering opportunities for product displays or for viewing the automated robotics labs. Classrooms and computer training facilities are located on the second floor with the instruction coordinators' offices and Skills Enhancement/Resources Center. Heavier training labs and shop areas are on the first floor providing on-grade access of equipment.

The materials and finishes used throughout the Training Center are aesthetically compatible with the industrial setting, yet very inviting for individual and group learning environments.

The UAW/Ford MnSCU Training Center provides maximum flexibility, not only for meeting today's needs, but also allowing for tomorrow's growth and change.

Opposite page from top, views of main entry and of south elevation.
Left from top, computer training center; main auditorium and main lobby.

Ohio Bureau of Criminal Identification and Investigation

London, Ohio, 1999

Client
Ohio Department of Administrative Services

Principal in Charge
Curtis J. Moody, FAIA

Project Manager/Designer
Timothy M. Colchin, AIA

Interior Designer
Jill Seitz

Construction Administrator
William C. Reinehr, EIT

Photographers
Leslee Kass, Todd B. Dove

Despite several previous additions to the Bureau headquarters, the organization considered yet another building addition to support its needs. Architects studied the conditions of the existing building and developed several expansion scenarios. After conducting a feasibility study, the designer recommended building a new headquarters facility, including a new DNA laboratory, on a different site.

The new 112,500 sq. ft. facility has a 40,000 sq. ft. DNA laboratory, a 20,000 sq. ft. Forensics laboratory, a state of the art fingerprint identification computer database, an indoor basement level firing range, and a new materials handling storage area. A significant challenge in this project was the coordination of complex mechanical, electrical, and plumbing systems, especially for the DNA and Forensics laboratories.

In addition to architectural and interior design services, civil engineers conducted a utility feasibility study designed for water, sanitary sewer services, and storm water drainage and detention, and providing parking areas for 177 vehicles on a 25-acre site.

This facility is the winner of a 2000 Associated Builders and Contractors, Inc. Award of Excellence.

Opposite page from top, views of main entry and of north elevation.
Left, high security reception area.
Below, entry atrium and monumental staircase.

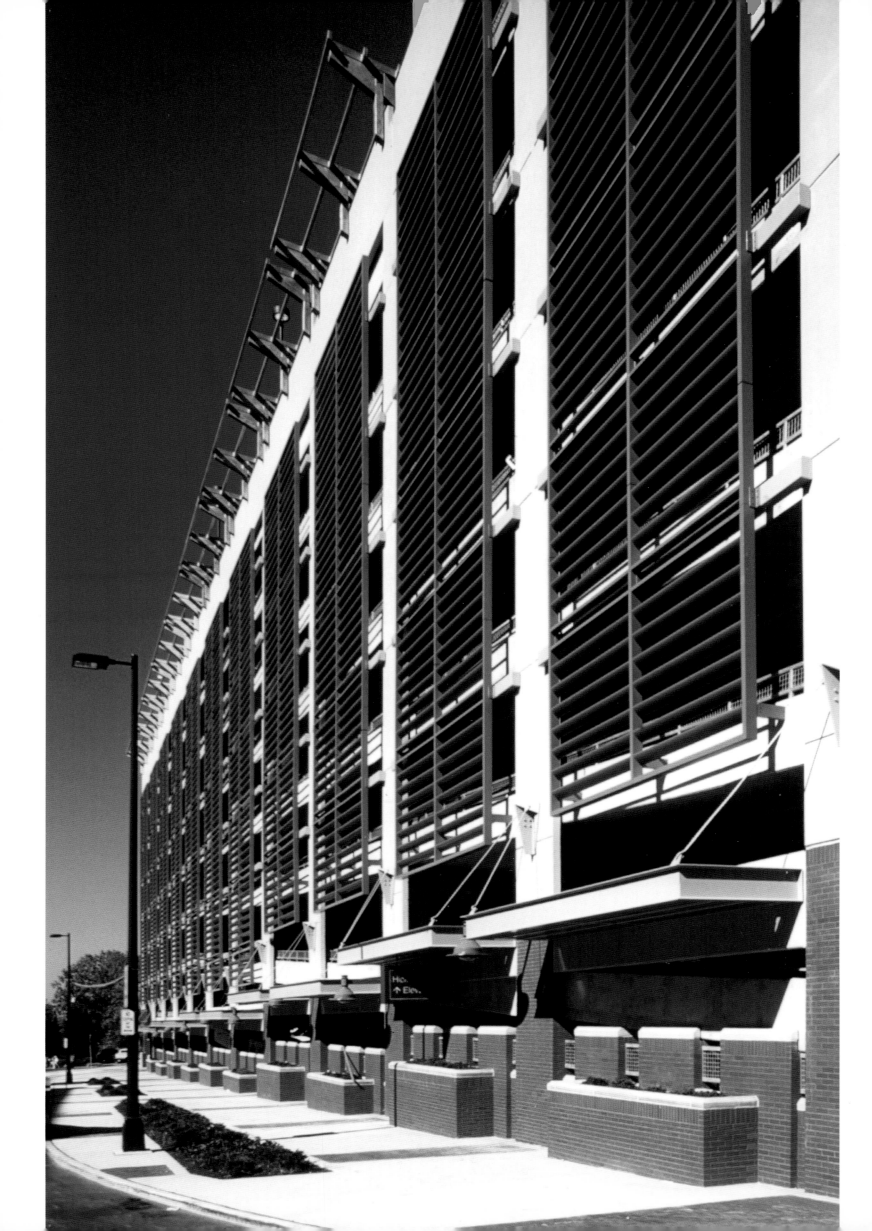

Nationwide Parking Garage

Columbus, Ohio, 2000

Client
Nationwide Insurance

Principal in Charge
Curtis J. Moody, FAIA

Project Manager
Harold Shrock, AIA

Project Assistant
Jim Sherer, AIA

Project Designer
Joaquin Serantes

Construction Administrator
Paul F. Pryor, AIA

Photographer
Michael Houghton,
Studiohio

The original parking garage for Nationwide Insurance was built in 1976 and was once the northwest border to downtown development in Columbus, Ohio. With the creation of a new downtown destination, "The Arena District," a pedestrian-oriented community alive with entertainment, the parking garage building is now an entrance to both the downtown area and the new thriving entertainment complex.

The parking garage expansion creates 1,600 additional parking spaces and new stair and elevator towers that meet the arena's requirements for weekend and evening parking.

A key design challenge was to enhance the architecture of the existing structure while integrating the new 550,000 sq. ft. addition. At one of the corners of the existing building, a new stair tower acts as the gateway to the Arena District. The addition of new canopies and stainless steel panels to the existing garage creates a more pedestrian friendly façade, while exposed steel framing gives the existing façade new life. Banners projecting from the building announce current or upcoming events to traffic entering the area.

While function determines the form of the addition, precast panels and louvers create the desired visual effect. Canopies and raised planting beds create a pedestrian-friendly edge leading from the downtown area into the active Arena District. The raised planting beds tie into the expansive landscaping of the corporate office building, while the stair and elevator towers serve as bookends to the building and identify the points of entry.

The parking garage renovation creates a strong architectural statement and provides an exciting new passageway leading in and out of downtown Columbus,

Moody • Nolan received a 2000 National Organization of Minority Architects (NOMA) Design Excellence Award for this renovation project.

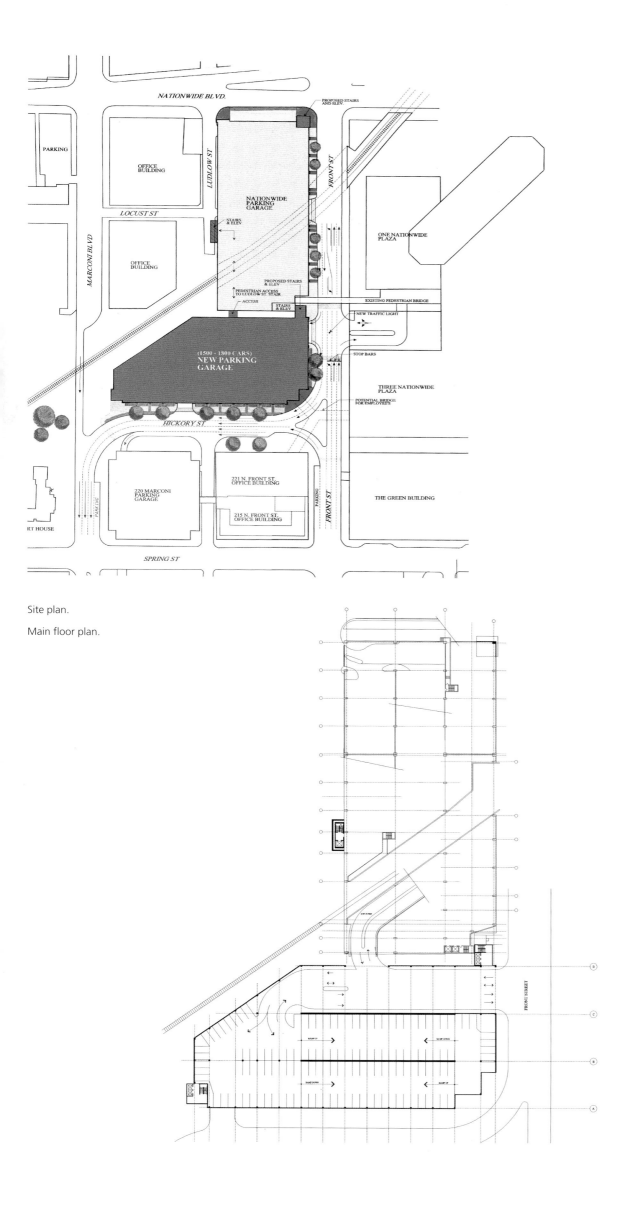

Opposite page top from left, view of parking streetscape along Marconi Avenue; central vertical circulation tower (view from Marconi Blvd.); tower at southwest corner of new parking garage. Opposite page bottom from left, vertical circulation tower at the corner of Nationwide Blvd. and Marconi Blvd.; view of parking garage from street entrance at Marconi Blvd.; presentation rendering of addition vertical circulation at the corner of Nationwide Blvd.

Site plan.

Main floor plan.

75

The Trumbull Center for Industrial Training and Education at the Kent State University, Trumbull Campus

Warren, Ohio, 2000

Client
Kent State University

Principal in Charge
Curtis J. Moody, FAIA

Project Manager
Ronald C. Minekime, AIA

Project Designer
Joaquin Serantes

Interior Designer
Caren C. Foster

Construction Administrator
William L. Kemper

Photographer
Todd B. Dove

This new 38,000 sq. ft. technology training center was developed in part to meet the retraining needs of automotive and steel workers displaced by computerized manufacturing technologies. This center also addresses training, noncredit, and degree programs that meet the particular needs of business, industry, and the physically challenged population in Northeast Ohio.

The facility is arc shaped and faces a second training building, triangular in design. Inside, there is a mix of classroom space and laboratory areas, some designed to accommodate the special training needs of this type of educational facility. For example, there are large bays for working on heavy machinery, and a paved space between the two training buildings provides an area for testing robotic and other manufacturing applications created in the laboratories and classrooms. Heavy machinery moves through the buildings and rolls out into the courtyard and back inside as needed.

The exterior is primarily brick and glass with the exception of a single protruding vertical aluminum panel. This detail designates a special place inside the building where a lecture hall with the latest audio-visual equipment is located.

The technology training center focuses on programs that address management, supervision, health and awareness issues, applications of computer and robotic technologies, and technology transfer as it relates specifically to industry, giving trainees and students the opportunity to study and apply the latest and most innovative computerized manufacturing technologies.

Opposite page from top, views of main entry and looking northeast.
Left, view looking south.

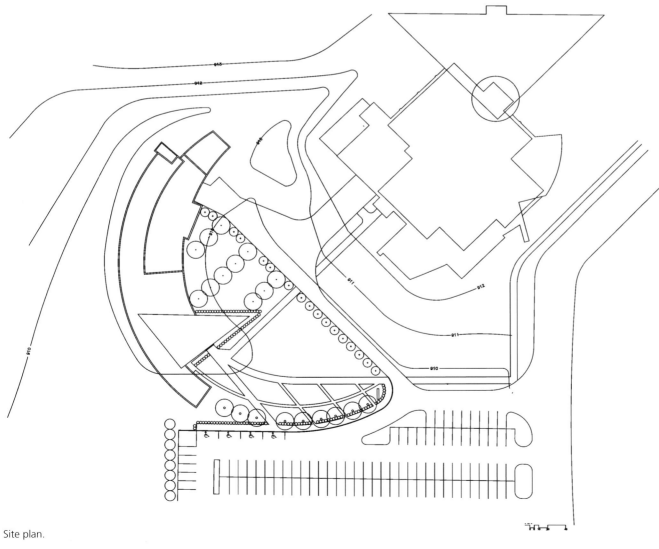

Site plan.

Top, view looking east.
Right, industrial
technology area.
Below, typical computer
classroom.

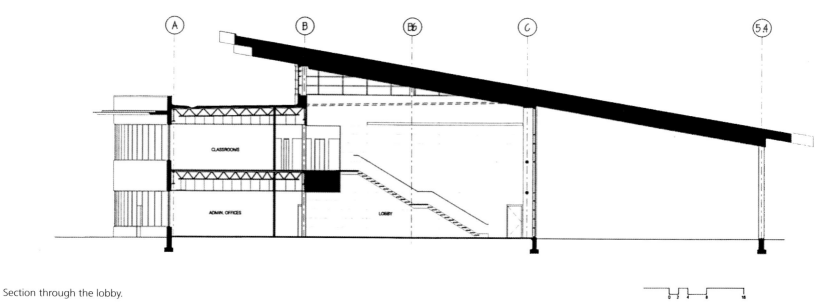

Section through the lobby.

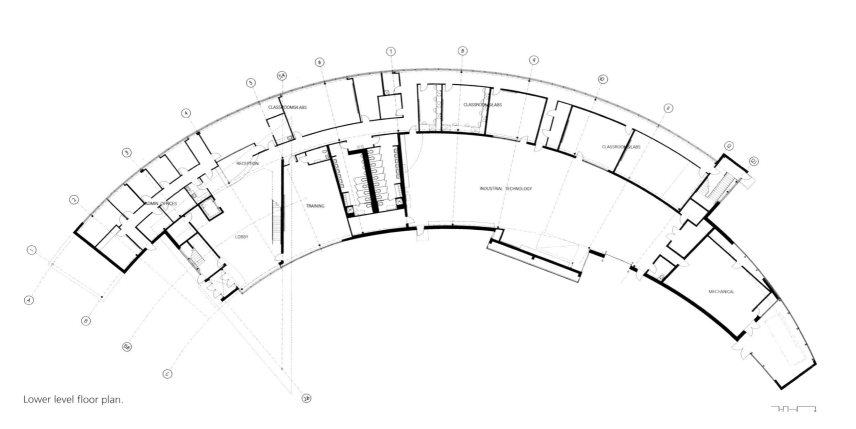

Lower level floor plan.

Student Life and Technology Center at Cincinnati State Technical & Community College

Cincinnati, Ohio, 2001

Client
Cincinnati State Technical & Community College

Principal in Charge
Curtis J. Moody, FAIA

Project Manager
Ronald C. Minekime, AIA

Project Designer
Joaquin Serantes

The three design goals for the Student Life and Academic Center were to create an outdoor student plaza for gathering, to build a parking structure, and to create an identifiable landmark for the College. In addition to the plaza and parking, the central space accommodates the culinary school, the information technology school, and the student life area, each having its own entrance and identity.

The edge of the limited land available for new construction dictated the form of the building and created an opportunity to meet the third goal of creating an identifiable landmark. The building stands 80 feet above the highway and creates an attention getting landmark and billboard for the College.

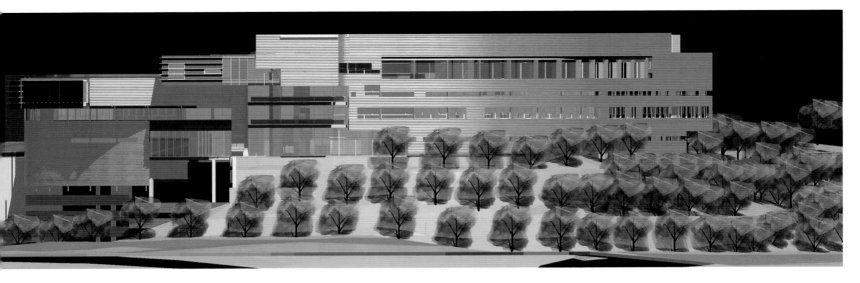

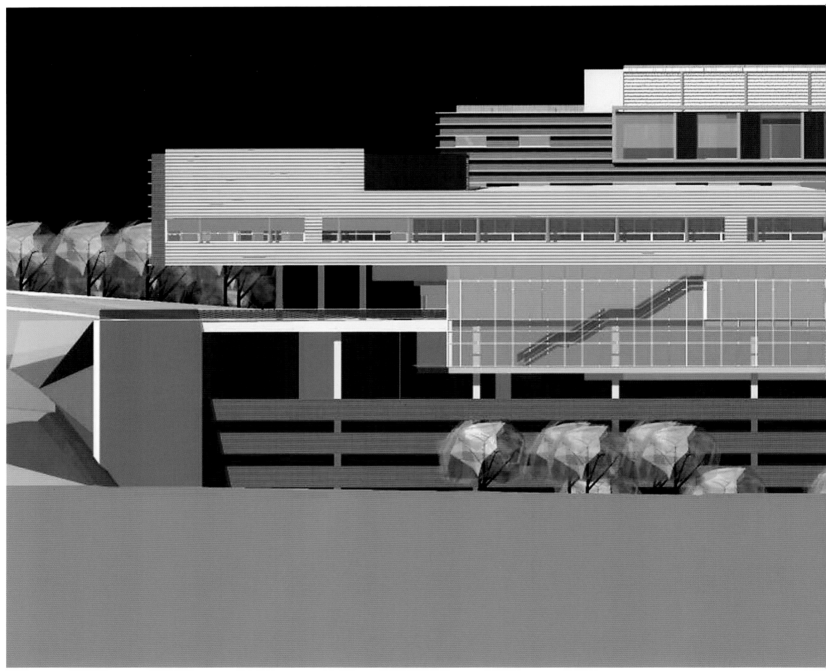

Opposite page, the curved reflective "skin" of the west elevation serves multiple purposes. The reflectability of the material and its detachment from the main structure creates a continuous shading device, while the irregular punctures echoes the motions of vehicles on I-75. This reflective skin morphises the building into a giant billboard.

Above, the structure is characterized by an extended horizontality achieved through shading devices and supported by existing campus context.

Left, the structure is purged on a hilltop and anchored by a parking structure cut into the hillside. The overhang of the suspended office "strand" reinforces the undulating nature of the plan and section.

Jesse Owens Memorial Stadium at The Ohio State University

Columbus, Ohio, 2001

Client
The Ohio State University

Principal in Charge
Curtis J. Moody, FAIA

Project Manager
Robert K. Larrimer, AIA

Project Architect
James K. Sherer, AIA

Construction Administrator
Arthur N. Cox

Photographer
Brad Feinknopf

Moody • Nolan and The Ohio State University (OSU) paid tribute to one of the world's most renowned athletes with the design of the Jesse Owens Memorial Stadium. The Jerome Schottenstein Center, another award winning design by this firm, included the Jesse Owens Memorial Stadium in its original master plan. The design goals of the stadium were to create a fitting memorial to Jesse Owens, a legendary athlete, and to provide a world class, modern facility for four varsity sports teams. In addition to supporting the needs of The OSU teams, the Jesse Owens Memorial Stadium meets all National Collegiate Athletic Association (NCAA) and Federation Internationale de Football (FIFA), the world's governing body for soccer's requirements. The stadium is one of the few collegiate athletic facilities specifically designed to balance the requirements of three field sports with track and field events.

Two tribute towers that flank the grandstand and mark the public points of entry are the focal points of the stadium. Historical photographs of the 1936 Olympic stadium where Jesse Owens was honored inspired the design for the tribute towers and the large concave discs that sit atop of them. The bases of the tribute towers function as ticket booths for events.

The grandstand accommodates 10,000 spectators and creates an elegant façade with exposed steel, brick arches, and piers that match the architecture of the nearby campus. Architectural elements mark the public entries and an aluminum picket fence encloses the entire facility. Located below the grandstand are concession stands, team offices, officials' locker rooms, and two team meeting rooms. An adjacent facility houses team lockers and showers and features a landscaped path connecting the two sites.

The stadium is visible from a major expressway and is a prominent piece of an overall athletic complex that includes an arena, ballpark, and indoor practice facility. The powerful imagery created by the architect has made this a remarkable memorial stadium and landmark in central Ohio.

This project was recognized with a 2002 Athletic Business Facility of Merit Award and a 2001 National Organization of Minority Architects (NOMA) Award of Excellence, and College Planning & Management Magazine featured The Jesse Owens Memorial Stadium as an example of a functional and creatively designed athletic center.

Right from top, views looking northwest and southeast.
Below left, press box.
Below right, view looking north through concourse.
Opposite page, view looking west.

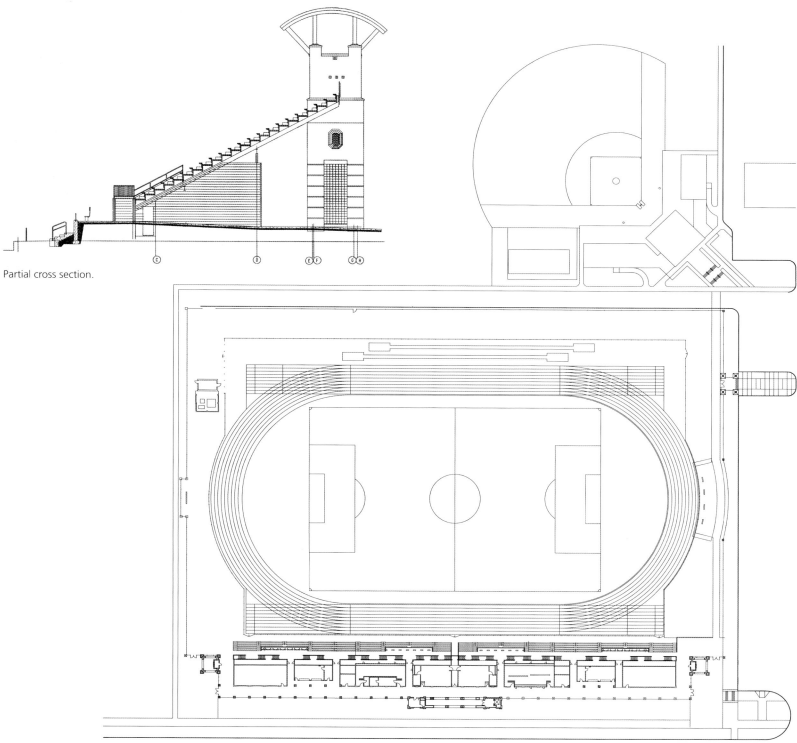

Partial cross section.

Site plan.

0 10 20 40 80

Student Center at Hampton University

Hampton, Virginia, 2001

Client
Hampton University

Principal in Charge
Curtis J. Moody, FAIA

Project Manager
Aaron Askew

Project Designer
Joaquin Serantes

Project Architect
Ronald C. Minekime, AIA

Interior Designer
Kimberly Blankenship

Construction Administrator
Arthur N. Cox

Photographer
Michael Houghton, Studiohio

Nestled at the edge of the intercoastal waterway, just a short airplane trip from places such as Washington, D.C. and New York City, this university provides students with a global educational culture. Yet the advantage of the university's location in Hampton, Virginia is only the beginning. An award-winning design, this 110,000 sq. ft. student center sets the nationwide standard for this type of facility.

The entrance lobby features an exciting three-story atrium with an elevated promenade overlooking a central grand stairway, the focal point of this impressive facility. Students find the central campus location convenient to their pedestrian cross-campus traffic. Upon entering the student center, students face the three-story atrium and promenade, while a 45 ft. by 140 ft. skylight floods the lobby with natural light, further enhancing the space.

A courtyard marks the intersection of the center's functions and student activities. Designed as a multipurpose student facility, activity areas include a 150-seat auditorium, a 900-seat conference center, fitness areas, a third floor indoor track, a food court, and a university retail shop. Student organization offices and deans' offices are located on upper floors. With its striking amenities, this student hub also serves as the president's preferred venue for hosting visiting dignitaries and special events.

The design of the building is contemporary and ecologically friendly. Brick ties the new structure to the existing campus building materials and traditional architectural styles. Large sections of curtain wall are composed of "green conscious" insulated e-glass glazing. The curtain wall interfaces with sections of two-story *brie soleil* sunscreen panels, providing solar screen and visual interest.

Approximately 10,000 sq. ft. of shell space was included in the initial build out.

Moody • Nolan received numerous awards for this project including, a 2002 School Planning & Management/College Planning & Management Education Design Showcase Award Winner for Outstanding Architecture and Design in Education, a 2002 American School & University (AS&U) Educational Interiors Showcase Student Centers/Service Areas award, a 2001 American Institute of Architects (AIA), Columbus Chapter, Merit Award and a 2001 National Organization of Minority Architects (NOMA) Award of Excellence.

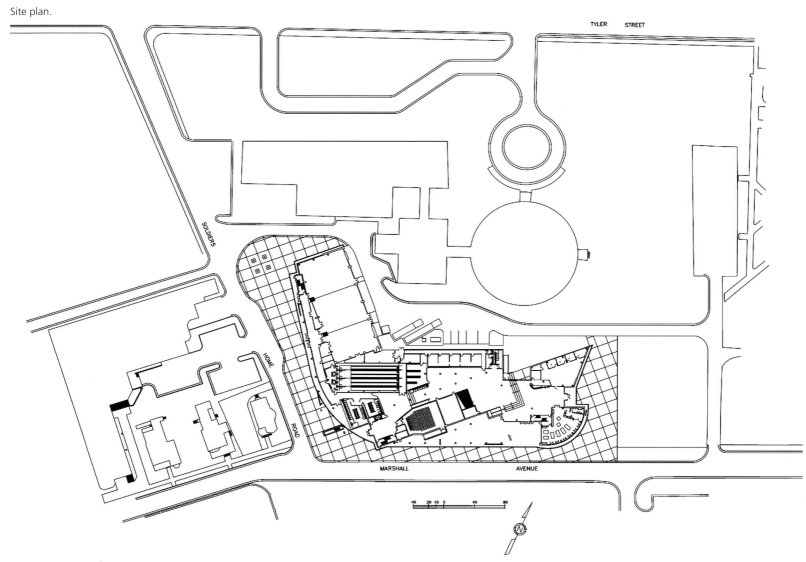

Site plan.

Opposite page, view of main atrium space from first floor.
Left from top, view of main atrium space from second floor; bowling alley and view of third floor fitness center.

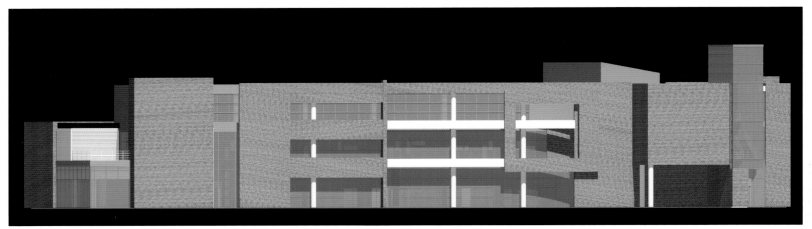

East and west elevations.

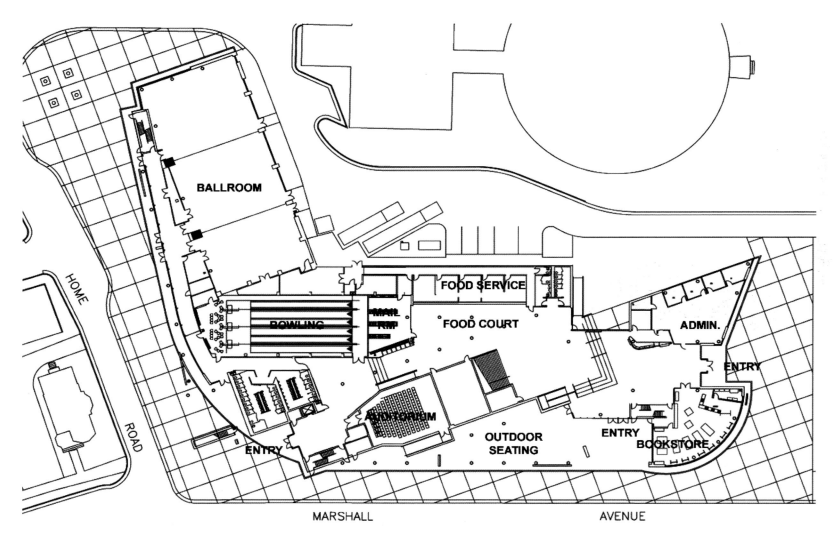

BALLROOM

HOME

ROAD

FOOD SERVICE

FOOD COURT

BOWLING

MAIL RM

ADMIN.

ENTRY

AUDITORIUM

ENTRY

OUTDOOR SEATING

ENTRY

BOOKSTORE

MARSHALL AVENUE

Main floor plan.

Left, the west facing *brise soleil* presents an intricate arrangement of opaque and transparent surfaces used as shading devices.

Below, transparency walls reinforce the students' connection to the surroundings while providing a place of repose.

Student Recreation Center at West Virginia University

Morgantown, West Virginia, 2001

Client
West Virginia University

Principal in Charge
Curtis J. Moody, FAIA

Project Manager
Mark J. Bodien, AIA

Project Architect
Marcus J. Brewer, AIA

Interior Designer
Eileen M. Goodman, NCIDQ

Construction Administrator
Dennis Keller

Photographer
Michael Houghton, Studiohio

Nothing could be more appropriate for the Mountaineers' student recreation center than the 50 ft. rock climbing wall soaring three levels high and lit by clerestory windows at the top that flood natural light into the deepest point of the building. The climbing wall is the heart of this 170,000 sq. ft. facility, home to intramural sports and recreational activities for the students, staff, and faculty of West Virginia University in Morgantown, West Virginia.

The designer facilitated several daylong planning sessions with University representatives prior to presenting three conceptual designs. Elements from each design were incorporated into the final design that culminated in a distinctive new gateway building.

The center, integrated into a tight sloping site, features a long internal public streetscape. The streetscape overlooks activity spaces that include 18,000 sq. ft. of exercise and weight lifting equipment, aerobics facilities, a walking/running track, lap and recreational pools, climbing wall, and racquetball, volleyball and basketball courts. Taking advantage of the spectacular setting, the center faces a nature area that remains visible from virtually all activity spaces inside. At night, the windows and lighting in the natatorium glow, creating a warm welcome for evening visitors. A juice bar and lounge area on different levels, a large central reception counter highlighted with glass art, and a *terrazzo* floor featuring abstract sports graphics complete the interior design.

The facility is completely accessible and maintains visually open spaces between activity areas. Fire separations protect the facility as mandated, and, despite the challenges of unusually stringent building regulations, do not block the view.

The exterior features sweeping curves, brick and split-face block walls, and soaring metal roofs that create a fifth elevation of gentle rooflines, visible from overlooking buildings. Energy-efficient translucent panels provide the gymnasium and climbing wall with natural light and reduce the demand for electricity during the day.

Funded by a student-approved tuition fee, this facility is a social hub and serves as a major recruitment and retention tool for the University.

This facility earned numerous awards including a 2002 School Planning & Management/College Planning & Management Education Design Showcase Award Winner for Outstanding Architecture and Design in Education, a 2002 American School & University (AS&U) Educational Interiors Showcase Physical-Education Facilities/Recreation Centers award, a National Intramural Recreation Sports Associations (NIRSA) Outstanding Indoor Sports Facilities Award, a 2001 American Institute of Architects (AIA), Columbus Chapter, Merit Award, and a 2001 National Organization of Minority Architects (NOMA) Special Merit Award for Design of Interior Space.

Opposite page from top, night view looking towards natatorium and secondary entry; view of leisure pool.

Left, the slopping glass entry, a glowing beacon at night, identifies one end of the entry concourse.

Below, the "free zone" passage through the building leads past views into activity areas and a central control desk.

Right, the curving forms are nestled into the hillside, minimizing the massiveness of the building and affording views from the fitness and pool areas over an existing pond and into a grove of trees.

Below, the "splash" of water from the leisure pool reaches up into the carpet and terrazzo of a lounge overlook area.

Opposite page from top, view from concourse looking at climbing wall and second floor track through interior glass walls; view from second floor track which overlooks climbing wall and basketball courts.

Right, view of 50 foot
climbing wall from
monumental stair.
Below, isometric
rendering.

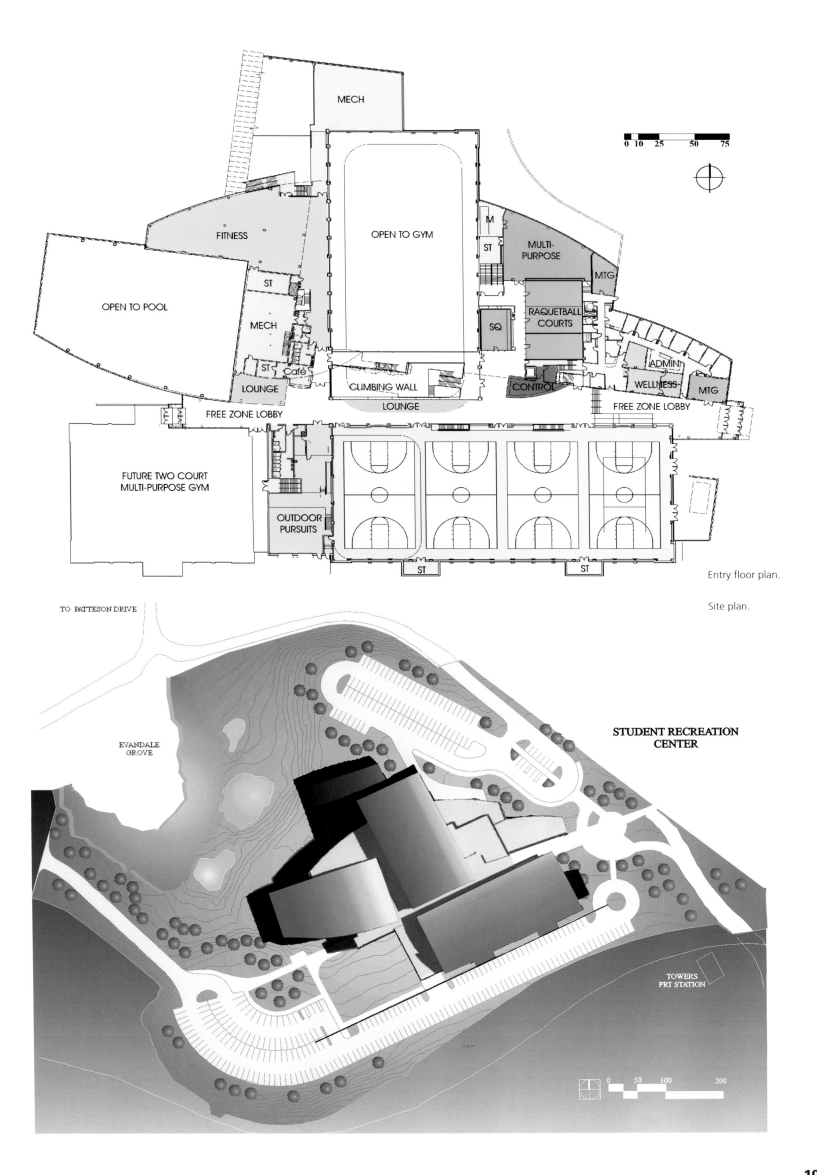

MECH

FITNESS

OPEN TO GYM

OPEN TO POOL

M

ST

MULTI-PURPOSE

MTG

ST

MECH

SQ

RAQUETBALL COURTS

ST

Café

CLIMBING WALL

CONTROL

ADMIN

LOUNGE

LOUNGE

WELLNESS

MTG

FREE ZONE LOBBY

FREE ZONE LOBBY

FUTURE TWO COURT
MULTI-PURPOSE GYM

OUTDOOR
PURSUITS

ST

ST

Entry floor plan.

Site plan.

TO PATTESON DRIVE

EVANDALE
GROVE

STUDENT RECREATION
CENTER

TOWERS
PRT STATION

0 10 25 50 75

0 50 100 200

Student Recreation Center and Field House at the University of Akron

Akron, Ohio, 2003

Client
University of Akron

Principal in Charge
Curtis J. Moody, FAIA

Project Manager
Mark J. Bodien, AIA

Project Manager/Architect
Ronald C. Minekime, AIA

Project Designer
Joaquin Serantes

Project Architect
Howard M. Blaisdell, AIA

Moody • Nolan, in association with TC Architects, and The Sports Management Group, is planning and designing this 286,000 sq. ft. student recreation/field house complex. The 138,000 sq. ft. student recreation center includes a three-court gymnasium, two-court multisport area, rock climbing wall, cardiovascular training area, free weights/strength training area, aerobics and dance studio, new leisure pool, and running/walking track. The 148,000 sq. ft. field house will include a varsity football practice field with a clearance of 60 feet, a six-lane indoor track, locker rooms, and related spaces. The facility also includes a 6,400 sq. ft. indoor varsity golf practice green and swing analysis space.

Right, site plan.
Below, north, west and
south elevations.
Opposite page,
perspective views of the
complex.

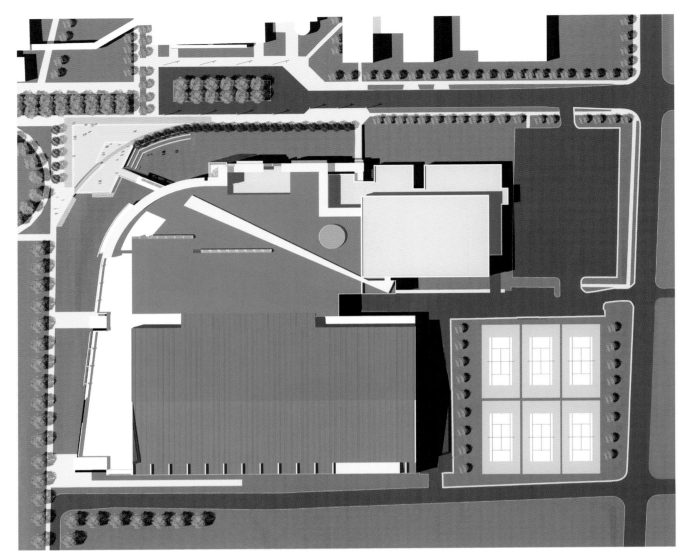

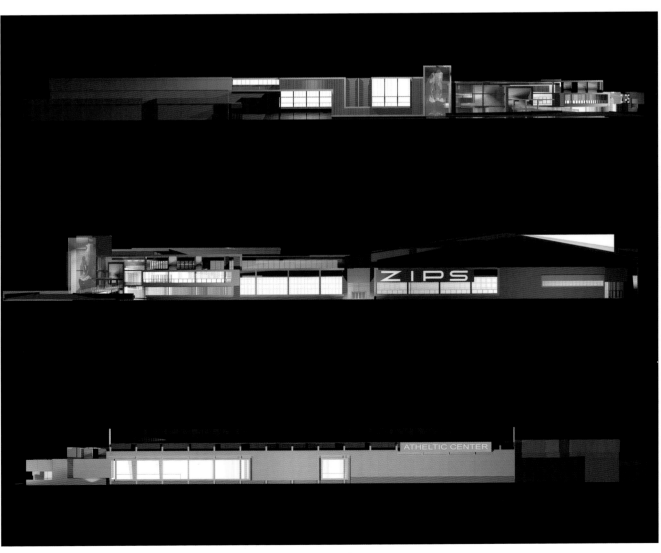

Entry level floor plan.

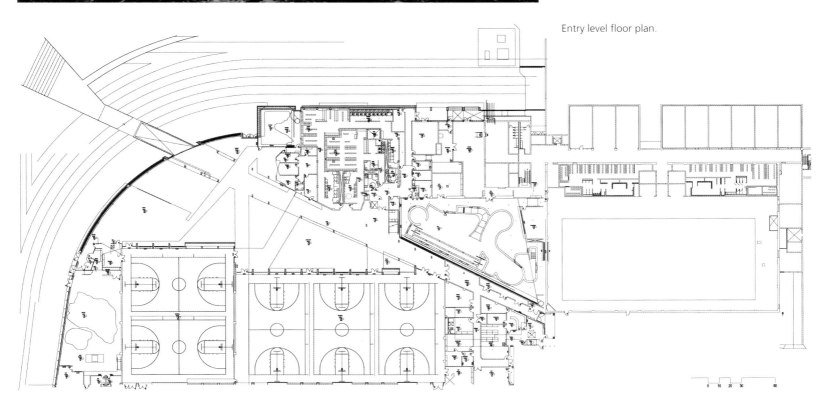

Right from top, the structure housing the climbing wall reflects the nature of its use; north to west elevation; early plan depicts competitive and diving pool addition and the master plans wishes of a strong pedestrian connection with the use of our free zone.
Opposite page top, aerial view of entry and student plaza (rock climbing structure in foreground).
Opposite page below, view of "free zone" from lounge area with fitness center below.

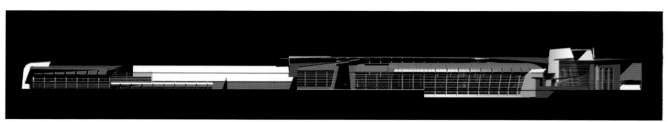

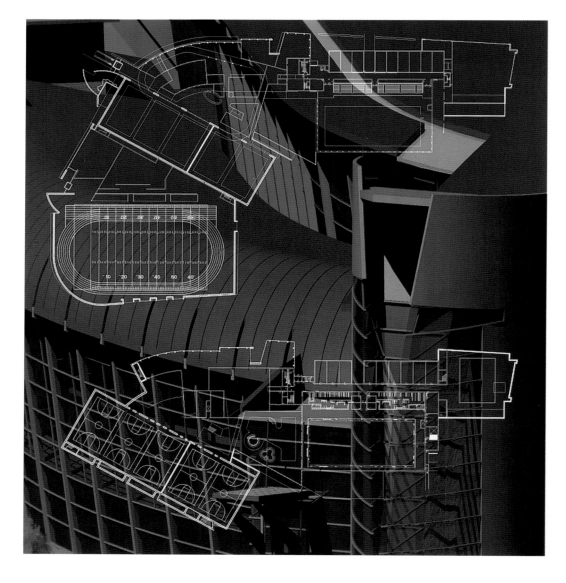

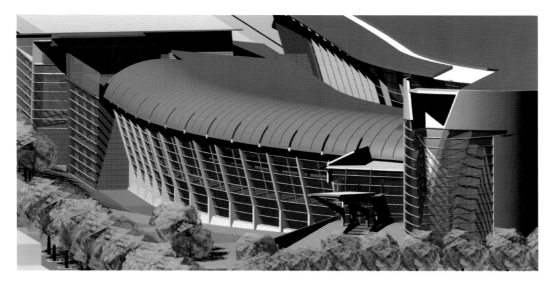

Larkins Hall at The Ohio State University

Columbus, Ohio, 2005

Client
The Ohio State University

Principal in Charge
Curtis J. Moody, FAIA

Project Designer
Antoine Predock, FAIA

Project Manager
Robert K. Larrimer, AIA

Project Coordinator
Craig Rutkowski

Sports Recreation Facilitator
Janet L. Jordan, CPRP

Interior Designer
Eileen M. Goodman, NCIDQ

Moody • Nolan, Architect of Record, and internationally acclaimed Antoine Predock, Design Architect, will design for the programmatic needs of Recreation Sports, the School of Physical Activity & Educational Services (PAES) and Athletics. When completed, this facility will be the largest collegiate recreational facility in the nation.

The new structure will house a completely new student recreation sports and fitness facility and all related classrooms, lab spaces, offices and support spaces. A new natatorium will replace the existing Peppe Aquatic Center. A redesigned outdoor recreation facility and the linkage of the facility to the greater campus are also included in the scope of the project.

Opposite page from top,
physical model of the
pedestrian bridge linking
the recreation center to
the academic building;
overview of Larkins
physical model.
Below left, computer
rendering of the
"satellite facility"
containing the outdoor
adventure program.
Below right, rendering
of the exhibition gym.

113

Cincinnati Public Schools Magnet Arts School

Cincinnati, Ohio, 2007

Client
Cincinnati Public Schools

Principal in Charge
Curtis J. Moody, FAIA

Project Manager
Timothy M. Colchin, AIA

Interior Designer
Eileen M. Goodman

Moody • Nolan leads the design effort for the team of Cole & Russel, Fanning/Howey Associates, Inc., for the new Cincinnati Public Schools Magnet Arts School. With $26 million in matching funds from the Cincinnati Arts Council, the new $52 million facility will match any high school performing arts facility in the country. When completed, this space will have 60 classrooms and accommodate up to 1,500 students. To promote the interaction of students, faculty, and professionals, the facility is located adjacent to the Cincinnati Music Hall.

This project earned a 2002 National Organization of Minority Architects Honor Award.

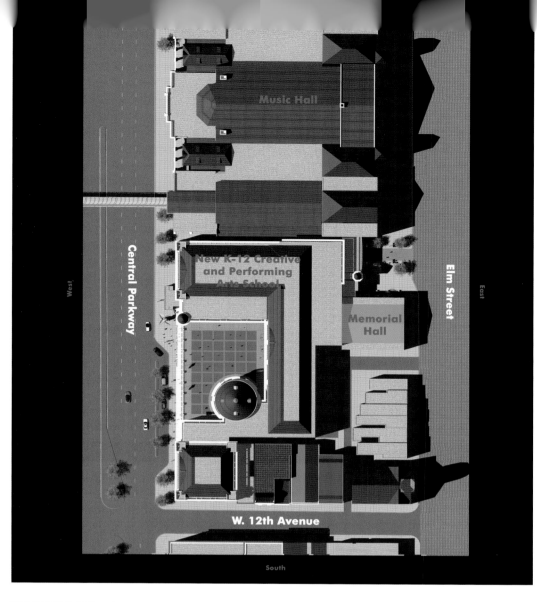

Opposite page from top, computer renderings showing view looking southeast from Central Parkway Street; night view looking east from across Central Parkway and west elevation of existing Music Hall and new Arts School.
Left from top, enlarged site plan and massing model of Art School and neighborhood context.

Selected Works

1982
New Life Apostolic Church
Columbus, Ohio

Ohio Reformatory for Women
Marysville, Ohio

1983
Medical Logistic Infill
Renovation and Addition
The Ohio State University
Columbus, Ohio

1984
The Martin Luther King Complex for Cultural
and Performing Arts
Renovation and Addition
Columbus, Ohio

1985
Muirfield Village Recreational Complex
Dublin, Ohio

Biggs-Woody Hayes Multi-Sport Complex
Renovation and Addition
The Ohio State University
Columbus, Ohio

Student Services Building
Central State University
Wilberforce, Ohio

1986
St. Paul A.M.E. Church
Redesign Interior Space
Columbus, Ohio

McPherson Stadium & Track
Central State University
Wilberforce, Ohio

1987
Karl Road Branch Library
Columbus, Ohio

Zion Center Museum
Renovation and Addition
Dayton, Ohio

Sawyer Towers
Multiple Family Housing Unit
Renovation
Columbus, Ohio

1988
Columbus Urban League Headquarters
Columbus, Ohio

Lucas County M. R. 484 Training Center
Warehouse Providing Training Work for Persons with
Developmental Disabilities
Renovation
Maumee, Ohio

Broad Street Bridge Over Alum Creek
Columbus, Ohio

1989
Maumee Bay State Park
Oregon, Ohio

Governor's Mansion
Renovation
Bexley, Ohio

1990
Public Services Administration Building
Lima Technical College
Lima, Ohio

Recreational Facility
Rio Grande Community College
Rio Grande, Ohio

1991
Recreational Sports Facility & Natatorium
Miami University
(In Association with HOK Sports)
Oxford, Ohio

Copeland Hall
Renovation and Addition
Ohio University
Athens, Ohio

James Thurber House
Historic Preservation
Columbus, Ohio

1992
Team Rahal Headquarters
Renovation
Hilliard, Ohio

Fort Hayes Metropolitan Education Center
Renovation
Columbus, Ohio

Greenbrier
Multi-Family Housing
Columbus, Ohio

1993
Dublin Community Recreation Center Phase I
Dublin, Ohio

Emergency Operations Center/Joint Dispatch Facilities
Columbus, Ohio

Highbanks Nature Center
Delaware, Ohio

Friendship Church
Columbus, Ohio

1994
1996 Olympic Preliminary Basketball Venue
Morehouse College
Atlanta, Georgia

Mt. Camel West
Renovation and Addition
Columbus, Ohio

Shiloh Baptist Church
Columbus, Ohio

1995
Police Precinct Prototype
Metropolitan Government of Nashville
& Davidson County
Nashville, Tennessee

The McConnell Heart/Health Center
Cardiovascular Clinic and Fitness Center
Columbus, Ohio

Base Civil Engineering Maintenance Facility
Ohio Air National Guard
Toledo, Ohio

Health Science Building
Master Plan and Redesign
Cleveland State University
Cleveland, Ohio

Student Services Building
Renovation
Franklin University
Columbus, Ohio

1996
Paul Robeson Cultural Center
Consulting Architect and Interior Design
Penn State University HUB (Student Center)
University Park, Pennsylvania

Medical Office Building
Surgery Replacement Center
Wooster Community Hospital
Wooster, Ohio

Trickel Office Building
Renovation
Orlando, Florida

Greater Columbus Convention & Visitors Bureau
Columbus, Ohio

1997
Smith Brothers Hardware Renovation
Headquarters for Retail Planning Associates
Columbus, Ohio

Children's Hospital Northwest Center
Dublin, Ohio

Napier Elementary School
Nashville, Tennessee

Longaberger Alumni House
Interior Design
The Ohio State University
Columbus, Ohio

Ohio School Boards Association Headquarters
Columbus, Ohio

1998
Heritage Park/Everal Barn
Listed on National Register of Historic Places
Restoration
Westerville, Ohio

Sunrise Communities (formerly Karrington
Communities)
Assisted Living Facilities
Interior Design
Various Locations

Columbus Metropolitan Housing Authority
Headquarters
Columbus, Ohio

Downtown Streetscape
City of Delaware, Ohio

Howard University Bookstore
Interior Design Renovation
Washington, D. C.

Police Precinct Substations
Columbus, Ohio

1999
Bentley Hall
Renovation and Addition
Ohio University
Athens, Ohio

Camp Perry Reservation
Ohio National Guard
Port Clinton, Ohio

Liberty Township YMCA
Powell, Ohio

Women's Hospital of Indianapolis
Indianapolis, Indiana

Chattanooga Recreation Centers
Programming and Conceptual Design
Chattanooga, Tennessee

Worthington Recreation Center
Addition
Worthington, Ohio

Student Center
Renovation and Addition
Hocking College
Nelsonville, Ohio

2000
Columbus Police Training Academy
Columbus, Ohio

Nashville International Airport & Operations Center
Relocation
Nashville, Tennessee

Northwest Detroit Youth
and Family Center
Design and Feasibility Study
Detroit, Michigan

Eagan Community Center
Planning and Design
Eagan, Minnesota

United Way
Childcare
Columbus, Ohio

City of Kent Main Fire Station Expansion
Kent, Ohio

2001
Oklahoma Indoor Athletic Training Facility
The University of Oklahoma
Norman, Oklahoma

Linden Elementary School
Columbus Public Schools
(In Association with Fanning/Howey Associates)
Columbus, Ohio

Beeghley Center Rehabilitation
Renovation and Rehabilitation
Youngstown State University
Youngstown, Ohio

Agler Green Apartments
Columbus, Ohio

Porter Hayes Elementary/Middle School
Planning and Design
Cincinnati, Ohio

Collaborative Projects
Vern Riffe Center/State Office Tower, 1984
In Association with Bohm-NBBJ
Columbus, Ohio

Columbus Convention Center, 1989
In Association with Trott Eisenman
Columbus, Ohio

State Capitol Restoration, 1990
In Association with Schooley Caldwell Architects
Columbus, Ohio

New Administration Headquarters, 1993
The Ohio Department of Agriculture
In Association with Maddox NBD
Reynoldsburg, Ohio

Hilltop State Lands Administrative Office Building, 1994
In Association with URS Consultants and Maddox NBD
Columbus, Ohio

Mall at Tuttle Crossing, 1994
In Association with developer The Taubman Company
Dublin, Ohio

Adelphia Coliseum, 1996
Football Stadium for the Tennessee Titans
In Association with HOK Sports
Nashville, Tennessee

Paul Brown Stadium, 1997
Football Stadium for the Cincinnati Bengals
In Association with NBBJ Sports & Entertainment
Cincinnati, Ohio

Center of Science & Industry (COSI), 1999
In Association with Bohm NBBJ and designer
Arata Isozaki
Columbus, Ohio

Principals
Curtis J. Moody, FAIA, NCARB
Robert K. Larrimer, AIA
Paul F. Pryor, AIA, NCARB
J. William Miller, AIA, ACHA
Eileen M. Goodman, NCIDQ
Alden M. McGee, PS
George E. Downing, PE
Valerie D. Klingman, PE, PS
Mark J. Bodien, AIA
Clyde R. Seidle, PE

Principal Emeritus
Howard E. Nolan, PE

Associate Principal
Steven C. Glass, AIA
G. Edward Alting, CSI
Elizabeth A. Thompson, AIA
David King, CPA

Senior Associates
Dennis Keller
Aaron Askew
Charles W. Tarr, AIA
Arthur N. Cox
Peter J. Kienle, FSMPS
Philip G. Wilson

Associates
Ronald C. Minekime, AIA
Rex W. Hagerling, AIA
Timothy M. Colchin, AIA, NCARB
Larry E. Pointer
James T. Eckstein, AIA
Caren C. Foster
Callie M. Porter
Howard M. Blaisdell, AIA
Jay Boone, AIA
Mark A. Brake
Todd B. Dove
M. Corazon Roush, AIA, AICP
Joaquin Serantes
Brian Tibbs
Don E. Rife, AIA, NCARB
Craig Rutkowski

Architecture
Brian Alting
Scott D. Baker
Michael J. Brendle
Marcus J. Brewer, AIA
Gregory Briya
Michael Burriss
Peter Cameron
Ronald Canini, AIA
Anthony Coalt
Marcia Rees Conrad, AIA
Shawn Conyers
Julie Cook
Daniel W. Delk, AIA
Erin Ditty
Jean P. Gordon, AIA, NCARB
Jon Guldenzopf, AIA, NCARB
Michael Hall
Kristen Harper
Kevin M. Holland
Robert Houser
Anup Janardhanan
Janet L. Jordan, CPRP
Ichiro Kameoka
Darren M. Kelly
William L. Kemper
John Kloch, RA
Cassandra Ladd
James W. Larkins, AIA
Woojin Lim
Jason L. Marciniak
Milan Moncol
Terrance Nash
Linda Nunnelly
Page Onge, AIA, NCARB
Wade A. Price, AIA
Alvin L. Reed, Jr.
William C. Reinehr, EIT
Harold Shrock, AIA
James K. Sherer, AIA
Patrick Stuart
Edward P. Thiell, AIA
Tim Traber
Jodi VanderWiel
Kelton Waller

Dynamic Media
Jeff Davis
Craig Rose
Chris Schwanekamp
Michael Smith
Alex Voltz

Engineering
Gregory Bachman, PE, PS
Paul H. Baumann, PE
Kathleen E. Dussault, PE
Amanda Engle, EI
Maher Girgis, PE
Anthony W. Golden
Berkley Hill, PE
Lori Hochradel
Charles Huff
Kelly Jordan
Mark Larrimer, EI
Rick Murray
Michael H. Rickard
Scott D. Seaman, EI
Alexander Tandetnitsky
George Tomashuk, PE
Fonda G. Welker, EI
Andrew D. Wolpert, EI
David A. Younger, PE

Interior Design
Kimberly Blankenship
Kathleine Cole
Brad Hammond
Janet L. Hines
Krysten Italiano
William W. Markland
David C. Miller
Janeen M. Peters, IIDA
Jill Seitz

Marketing
Danielle M. Ford
Jenifer Pfeiffer
Sondra S. Smith

Administrative
Michele Allen
Tova Black-Durant
Debbie Burley
Karen Gary
Clarence Miller
Curtis Miller
Jessica Miller
Brent Segner
Jody Tenzos
Shannan Wheaton
Shannon Wilkins
Lauren I. Williams
Lloyd Zook